A Bill of Rites,

A Bill of Wrongs,

A Bill of Goods

Also available from the University of Nebraska Press

Conversations with Wright Moris (BB 630)
Edited with an introduction by Robert E. Knoll

WRIGHT MORRIS

A Bill of Rites,

A Bill of Wrongs,

A Bill of Goods

UNIVERSITY OF NEBRASKA PRESS
Lincoln and London

Publishers on the Plains

UNP

Copyright © 1967, 1968 by Wright Morris
Preface to the Bison Book Edition copyright © 1980 by the University of Nebraska Press

The lines by T. S. Eliot on the quotation page are from "Little Gidding" in Four Quartets, copyright, 1943, by T. S. Eliot. Reprinted by permission of Harcourt, Brace & World, Inc.

The lines on page 131 are from "Among School Children" and are reprinted with permission of The Macmillan Company from Collected Poems by William Butler Yeats.
Copyright 1928 by The Macmillan Company, renewed 1956 by Georgie Yeats.

First Bison Book printing: 1980

Most recent printing indicated by first digit below:
1   2   3   4   5   6   7   8   9   10

Library of Congress Cataloging in Publication Data

Morris, Wright, 1910–
   A bill of rites, a bill of wrongs, a bill of goods.

   Reprint of the ed. published by New American Library, New York.
   I.   Title.
[PS352.07475B5   1980]   814'.52   80–389
ISBN 0–8032–3065–6
ISBN 0–8032–8107–2 pbk.

Reprinted by arrangement with the author

Manufactured in the United States of America

AGAIN AND AGAIN
FOR JO

Preface to the Bison Book Edition

These pieces were written in the mid-sixties, to relieve my accumulating exasperation with *how things were*. How they were was summarized in the opening essay, "A Museum of Happenings," where we find this comment.

> At the moment when the writer never had it so good, his works available at the price of a sandwich, the sandwich may prove to be the public's better buy. . . . No bill of rites will silence or appease our hunger for more of the facts than we possess: no bill of goods supplies us with an illusion commensurate with our needs. The one frontier unexplored is our diminishing consciousness.

How will the reader of the eighties feel about these historical abuses? Have they changed, or gone away—or have we merely become accustomed to them? Here is a comment by Robert Coles in a review of Christopher Lasch's *The Culture of Narcissism.*

> When a sense of the past or the future is either attenuated or lost, what is left but an endless series of fads?

vii

This reflects the perspective of ten years on the enthusiasms of the sixties. We had new ones in the seventies, of course, but we were somewhat more aware of their transient nature. When I sample the pages of *A Bill of Rites* I am impressed and amused by the author's fearless indignation. Such indignation relies on the feeling that injustice, or folly, will cease, once it is pointed out. The loss of such indignation can be described as the downward path to wisdom.

And the upward path to wisdom? Perhaps it is best captured in this statement of Ludwig Wittgenstein.

My aim is to teach you to pass from a piece of disguised nonsense to something that is patent nonsense.

Is it patent nonsense that strains indignation so that it fails to contain the writer's exasperation? Words bring temporary relief, but no cure. What I sought for was the immediacy of the viewer who stops to watch hotcakes cooking in a restaurant window, where the blending of sight, smell, and hunger has both its appeal and its nausea. Let the interested reader judge for himself the relevance of how things once were, to how they still are.

WRIGHT MORRIS
Mill Valley, California
December 1979

CONTENTS

What was the case but magnificent
for pitiless ferocity?

HENRY JAMES

Second, the conscious impotence of rage
At human folly, the laceration
Of laughter at what ceases to amuse.

T. S. ELIOT

A Bill of Rites,

A Bill of Wrongs,

A Bill of Goods

I: *A Museum of Happenings*

My aim is to teach you to pass from a piece
of disguised nonsense to something that is
patent nonsense.

LUDWIG WITTGENSTEIN

Three years ago I cast my vote for a President the
computers had already elected. The polls had predicted it:
the computers confirmed it. The decisive factor in my role
as a voter was my position in the Pacific time zone of the
republic. The issues were settled before I cast my vote. A
handful of diehards, caught in the wrong time zone but
determined to influence the course of history, complained
about casting their vote after the election was over, but to
correct this detail was no easy matter. Millions of dollars
had been spent to achieve instant news, and the news was
that the election was over. The earth, to place the blame
where it belonged, simply rotated too slowly. It had not —
as I had not — kept abreast of the times. Modern man in
the wrong time zone was obsolete. Was it my vote, or my
nature, that proved to be expendable?

We say that's *how things are.* And how are they? That

3

is precisely what escapes us. The Emperor acts strangely, but we still behold him in his old clothes. In the emergence of new forms, or the breakdown of old forms, the first blurring of essential and established distinctions will occur between our ideas of life and art, of facts and imagination. In the opinion of some artists the distinctions have already disappeared. Art and life are interchangeable parts. Life — if one can just grasp it — will prove to be enough. Allen Kaprow comments: "Once the task of the artist was to make good art: now it is to avoid making art of any kind."

A young artist, Frank Gallo, adds: "I don't believe in art: I am not even interested in art. I keep my work free of esthetic judgements."

A century earlier Walt Whitman observed: "No one will get at my verses who insists upon viewing them as a literary performance, or attempt at such performance, or as aiming mainly toward art of estheticism."

So it is not a new rebellion. The artist who believes himself in chains, real or imaginary, speaks in this manner. He rejects something, he may destroy something, to set his mind free. In making it new, he hopes to start from scratch. This longing is more profoundly felt among the painters, where the mania for newness, for sonic-boom breakthroughs, generates more heat than light, but it is also revealed in the writer's misgiving, in theory and practice, of the ultimate truth of imagination. The novelist feels this disquiet. The nonfiction novel reflects the disorder. Now that the heart is an interchangeable part, the heart's affections may be harder to account for, and the testimony of Keats, "I am certain of nothing but the holiness of the heart's affections and the truth of Imagination," has lost its old persuasion.

Uncertainty on both of these points we know to be characteristically modern. Imagination daily gives way to *the facts:* affections judged holy are the first we find suspect. But neither the heart's affections nor the imagination are so easily jettisoned. Although the artist may feel he has altered with the times, and inwardly changed profoundly, in the mercurial world of fiction and fact he represents one of the constants. He is an artist. He does not change so easily as he thinks. He will be among the first to become something else, and he will be among the last to hold fast to what is passing. Two lines from Beckett's *Molloy* describe his situation: "From things about to disappear I turn away in time. To watch them out of sight, no, I can't do it."

He is at once avant-garde and reactionary. One part of his nature feels the chill of death, the creeping cold in the extremities: the other hails the dawn of a new age. This is not a happy time to be an artist, but it is even worse not to be one. He *is* how things are. His function is to sound out how he is.

In the audience a change of considerable importance is the proportion that consider themselves to be artists. They assemble not merely to see how he is doing, but how soon they will be doing it themselves. The cannibalism long common among researchers and scholars is now a new element of the art scene. The artist who takes off can expect to be knocked off: the output is directly wired to the in-put. The results of this in-breeding fill one of the wings of *communications,* a testimonial to the new participating audience. It has inspired Marshall McLuhan to heights of science fiction, and all of us to digestion or regurgitation. In communications there are no off-limits. We are ingesting or digesting. If the current is on, we are all a participating audience. Mr. McLuhan puts it like this: "As the audience becomes participant, involved in the total electric drama, it can become a major work force: and the classroom, as much as any other place, can become a scene in which the audience can perform an enormous amount of work."

Most artists would say so far so good. What has often been modern in modern art is the amount of work it demands of the participant. Some participants have gone on record as working harder than the artist. Mr. McLuhan quotes Robert Oppenheimer as saying, "There are children playing in the street who could solve some of my top problems of physics, because they have modes of sensory perception that I lost long ago."

If that is true, Mr. Oppenheimer had an out that most artists do not. His point brings us to a nice but crucial distinction between science and art. The artist hopes to retain a child's sensory perceptions, but they will solve no problem for him. He himself, not the audience, must still do the work.

Nothing seems farther from Mr. McLuhan's mind than what he actually finds himself describing. Adolf Hitler, for example, once a part-time artist, grasped the principles of audience participation with uncanny intuition. The total drama we call war is difficult to conjure up without them. Yet nothing seems farther from Mr. McLuhan's short-circuited mind. It is part of our obsession, as moderns, to solve insoluble problems with formulas and feedbacks, wherein we all hope to participate in the electric drama of discovery. In coming of age, communications has become an end in itself.

To the extent that we know this, accept it or distrust it, contribute to it, tolerate it, or merely resent it, we are contemporaries and speak the same Newspeak. Like it or not, we are a participating audience. When we say, "That's how things are," it's what we mean. We're in it. We are all wired for sound. Mr. McLuhan's exaltation seems to come from the tingling these wires give his extremities, but some of us look for more in drama than twinkling toes. Can we predict that facts, projected in living color, will one day replace fiction on the late, late show? After all, who needs fiction? What could be stranger than the news on the hour?

It is a matter of time — that is prime time — before a parent, or a sweetheart, getting the news from Huntley, will glance up to recognize the smile, or the gesture, or the face of a soldier as vaguely familiar.* When the camera zooms in for the shock of recognition, that is what it will be. The war is already covered by the networks better than the war department: the participating audience covers the war for itself. Thousands fight it. Numberless millions sit in on it. As a continuing serial, war goes far toward solving the networks' major programming problems. A story without end. A cast of millions. An international theatre in the round. Seen as a game, the game of war need not wait for weekend billing. It gets prime time. We can predict its appearance on the late, late show. There is always something playing in the theatre of war.

Is it possible that total communications will prove to have the power total censorship lacked? The power to dispense with fiction, excommunicate art? To silence and dilute it with *communications* — a jamming of the air waves, the sight waves, the thought waves. The ceaseless, mindless massaging of the senses, the liquidation of si-

* The first such incident was reported in May 1967, under the caption PARENTS SEE SON WOUNDED. Mrs. A. Landon Morrow was watching a late news program on television. "Come quick, Landon," she cried, "here's our son!" The camera had focused briefly on Spec. 4 Landon Morrow, Jr. "I'll never forget the night I saw that," said Mrs. Morrow. "It was on WSB, Channel 2, April 30th, at 11 P.M."

lence, the drugging of reflection, the appropriation of the total mind in the electric drama of information? Nor need it be *information*. A surfeit of art, a prodigality of "artists," a glutting of the market with creators and the creative, may inspire in some a transport of participation but have a depressing effect on the artist. Is it safe to say they will be the artists who count? That no human being can be found, or described, as *un*creative has not merely jammed the lines of communication but generated in the artist a distaste for his calling. To be one of a suffocating creative crowd dims what is central to his function. His uniqueness. His assurance that the artist is one of a kind. In the abuse of art as therapy the creative act is one of merchandising. "Creative" advertising is intuitively structured to meet this need.

Understandably, the artist who deals with facts has few, if any, communication problems. Facts are facts: the public is expected to judge them for itself. The documentary war, the documentary novel, the documentary program deal with the facts. Fiction goes against the grain of the all-American mind. The audience has always shared this ingrained preference — what is new is to find it shared by the artist. When Truman Capote — we might say, of all people — speaks his piece about the new, nonfiction novel, we know it is the facts, not the fiction, that pay off. The look of *real* life is what we've always wanted, and the look of *real* life is what we're now getting. Many find it impossible to distinguish between real life and real Pop Art. Nor is it a small problem. Pop Art tableaus illustrate our daily quota of news. The gap between the ivory tower and the traffic tower has been narrowed by the long boom of the camera, and by the fiction that only the news comes to terms with life. Mr. Capote's new fictions, the war's old happenings, the museum of artifacts we recognize as Pop

Art, testify — so we believe — to how things really are. The holiness of some affections may still be in order, but the imagination is in disorder. The real world is realer, on the hour, by day — sur-realer by night.

Some years ago a candor-loving colleague asked me to spend an evening at his institution. He and his friends, he said, would like to "pick my brains." How say it better? How come to terms with what has been said? So far has table talk progressed since the days of Coleridge and Hazlitt. The spirit of the Donner party hovers over those conclaves where the midnight oil is fed with human fat. When we say *Genius Burning,* it is what we mean. No other word describes this voracity, this appetite, so well as cannibalism. Malice may whet it, but the lust derives from appetite. The rapacity of Hemingway toward "old" friends may partially arise from his sense of being threatened: *The Old Man and the Sea* conveys this message graphically. It is not an old story at all, but a new one: not the *work* of a lifetime, but the life itself that is now threatened. Publish or perish is the law of the jungle in the Groves of Academe. With the museums and archives of the past looted, the researcher turns to, or rather on, the present. The writer or the scholar with a brain to be picked must master the shell game of concealed resources. The publication that forwards his interests may exhaust both himself and his subject. The open-ended project, the unfinished dissertation, is one answer to the threat of premature liquidation. The new commandments are light on fornication, but they come down hard on communication. Thou shalt, for the Lord thy God is a hungry God.

It is characteristic that the next step before us so often proves to be the one behind us. We describe this bit of gamesmanship as *the last frontier.* It changes monthly.

Currently it is thought to be the mind. Man is fearfully and wonderfully made, but who would venture the opinion that he is bottomless? Already the sounds we hear in the night are the nails of the computer scratching the bottom of the barrel. Is it the great unknown that generates this fever, or merely the researcher's mania for data? With shame in his voice a science writer has confessed that we *still* don't know the secret of life. It may come as a shock to learn that life, any life, still has one. A secret. Something of which it might be deprived. What proves to be compulsive in the pursuit of knowledge is not relieved by the accumulation of data. Quite the contrary. This computer fodder merely increases appetite. The researcher is only appeased by further research.

The anthropologist Claude Lévi-Strauss, speaking of recent pre-Incan findings, commented, "This could open up new fields of speculation." New fields of speculation! One can feel his relief as a scientist. As material resources are uncovered and depleted, there will still be speculation. Endless. More inexhaustible than space.

From a seat too close for comfort, I once observed an "entertainer" drink the contents of several fish bowls crowded with goldfish, then regurgitate — as if untouched — all that he had swallowed. Goldfish leaped from the trout stream of his mouth. A remarkable act. I never thought I would see its like again. But the swallowing of more than a bowl of goldfish has become a commonplace matter, and the regurgitation is sometimes classed as a work of art. The current creative scene, and some of its creators, specialize in gorging and upchucking. The more revolting the performance, the better the press. It has been found that the mind can be emptied as easily, and to better effect, than the stomach. There is more in it. Nobody knows what might turn up. Now that to throw up is to speak up, it can be billed as a creative act. It is a gift, and has been recognized as such. This is, of course, an intellectual game and intellectuals naturally excel at it. They have more in the bucket, so to speak, and need the relief. Some do it the hard way, with much strain and gagging, others with the expertise of Susan Sontag. Just plain chucking up has seldom, if ever, been done with such felicity. Her performance features some of the drama of the seance: some are called up for burial, others resurrection. There is this creative upsurge, and there it is. To my limited knowledge Miss Sontag is the first to introduce genitalia to the field of reporting, and to note with such detail how and where the President scratches himself. This same sharp eye has led her to observe that America was founded on genocide, and that the white race is the cancer of human history. After such a performance we can only assume that she feels much better. The violation of the mind in the guise of ventilation — such as we find in the probing of Norman O. Brown — leaves it in a not dissimilar ravaged condition to the intestines after a dose of sulpha. Everything that is good and life-sustaining, along with the infection, has been removed. The cure recommended is worse than the disease. That might serve as a description of the panaceas suggested, on the one hand, by the hippie — the love potions and trips of the flower people — and the self-abuse of the intellectual who thinks to change history with purgatives. Between this type of "involvement" and the psychedelic dropout there is little to choose. There are ways to explain, but no way to assess, the effect of such abuses on the present, not to mention the long, tormented ascent of man.

In the emerging hippie culture the cast changes hourly, but the scene is still at Haight-Ashbury, in San Francisco.

The search for kicks, inherited from the beats, has obscured an urgent need of the hippie psyche. Depressed by the world of squares, the hippie begins with a diminished consciousness: understandably he seeks the quickest and easiest way to expand it. This is supplied by "acid." The "trip" is unmistakable internal assurance that he has expanded, and that he has arrived. The availability and cheapness of the drug is the distinguishing factor between the hippie and the beat. Not mere consciousness, but the world itself, *out there*, expands. The pangs (if any) of his cultural withdrawal provide a matchless background for the new order. He had not expected a "retinal circus" to replace the culture merry-go-round he had abandoned. It exceeds, to put it literally, his wildest dreams. Nor is it a fault of his own if more than twenty million people prove to be as young, or younger, than he is, strongly inclined to "tune in, turn on, and drop out."

The hippie scene is less exclusive than the beat scene, and its lines are harder to establish. There are weekend hippies. There is the hippie who blends, like the colors of madras, with the surrounding world of squares, or promotes the latest in Twiggy fashions. The time may soon be approaching when he will experience the only kick for which he is ill prepared. It is interesting to speculate what will happen when he tunes in on his first dry martini, and experiences the strange, rocky euphoria of the cocktail hour. That will be new. Like anything so new and far out it will spread. Already we have that mystifying problem as to what becomes of *old* hippies — could it be that they have rediscovered the lost world of the squares? The full circle of this syndrome will be complete when the alcoholic hippie, put into dry dock, is treated with LSD to put him back on his feet.

Seen through the peephole at the service entrance, like

the food slot at the back of a diner, audience participation
is the gloss we give to an insatiable process of appropriation. Anything that we can transform into information is
subject to appropriation. It lies in that expanding province
of "eminent domain." Once appropriated, it is then pro-
cessed for communication. No rocket goes up but what
something called data comes raining down. The word
communication is the respectable term that sustains and
justifies this astral harvest, but the word *liquidation* is
more clinically accurate. Indeed, it seems the function of
communications to liquidate information. The audience,
functionally speaking, is a Dispoz-all, with a gluttonous
appetite for information. This unflattering image is improved if we substitute the word *communications:* it is
remarkably transformed if we describe it as *education.*
The end result is the same: liquidation and increase of
appetite.

Thanks to what has come to pass, certain facts seem
clear. It is the nature of data to be liquidated, a job that
will soon be taken over by computers. It is the nature of
experience to elude liquidation in the guise of art. The
great stress on art — in a period suffocating with facts,
research, and information — suggests that although most
of us are crazy, not all of us are stupid. We know life from
death. We have an instinct for the bones that live. This
knowledge might prove to be sufficient to earn us Mr.
Eliot's forgiveness. Thanks to the computer the artist has
more time for prayer. He can cultivate his gifts for revelation, liquidate his burdens of information. He need not
know it all, merely master what little he knows. His audience will intuit, just as he does, the old distinctions between data and experience, between the bones merely,
and the bones that live.

The appropriation of the known, the liquidation of the

unknown, are cultural activities we never question. We assume it is always in the public interest, and increasingly of interest to the public. What we cover is subordinate to the fact that we are covering it. *Lunacy,* once thought to be a frailty of women, is now a madness peculiar to man: the heavens are currently the new theatre of the absurd. There is no accounting for tastes, but how many of us are enchanted by the poetry of the space program? Is it the gorge or the heart that rises from the pad at Cape Kennedy — is it the "coverage" or the program that has sold this moonshine to the public? Our words fly up, but our thoughts remain below. I do not mean to belittle the science of it, just the mania: a new front on an old familiar agony. Just a century ago it was called Romantic, and held its sway over poets and painters: its principles are now the sacred texts of the laboratory. Crack through or crack up in the hallow'd, disordered name of truth.

The space rush is currently a distraction from the last of the earthbound targets: *privacy.* In the expanding world of communications it is one of the few things left to feed on. The word itself admits to the fact that something is concealed. As such, it lies in the eminent domain of the news. We are inclined to see it as a treasured possession taken from us by force, stealth, cunning, the persuasion of large publisher advances, or siphoned from us by gadgets concealed in cocktail olives or the molars of a gorgeous blonde. This impression is nostalgic. It is a property and has its price. Many have found it baffling that several hundred couples recently exercised their sexual prowess under what we call scientific observation. For these people — of all ages — privacy was little more than unshared information, data waiting to be made into news. To be of service, to reveal and expose, to contribute to the machinery of communication, is a greater source of gratification to the lonely crowd than the imponderable sensations of privacy. What good is it? It makes news. The liquidation of privacy is a personal contribution to the expanding empire of communications: their motto might be, They also serve who publicly copulate.

In terms of the participating audience this might be considered something of a milestone. *Are you kidding?* is the label we give to those facts that defy classification. Sick humor licenses the sick man to share his illness with an audience. Thanks to communications audience participation is epidemic. No virus travels with the speed of the very sick joke. Appropriated in Brooklyn, exploited over Chicago, it can look forward to a West Coast diaspora, followed by liquidation or transformation. The bumper strip joker begins with GOD IS DEAD, soon followed by GOD IS ALIVE AND HIDING IN ARGENTINA, this in turn by GOD IS ALIVE AND IN THE WHITE HOUSE.

In the space of a few days the audience has appropriated this material and improvised upon it. Anyone on a cruise, or down with the flu, or with the TV out of order or the car repossessed, might have missed the performance. What you had to say may be old before you say it. Making the scene increasingly demands that we make it new.

The promise and the dilemma of appropriation are dramatized in the example of Picasso. It has been his genius to take whatever he can use. In this hunger and its appeasement he has become our most representative figure. Make it new. If you can't make it new, at least make it your own. It would seem to depend on the public's point of view if this is an act of creation or plagiarism. Is he creating or appropriating? It is merely part of talent for those with genius: something described as knocking off for those without it. In the current jousting scenes of art, knocking off has come to be an accepted practice. The sculptor ransacks the bathroom and the attic, the painter selects a basket of canned goods. An impalpable line appears to separate the man who makes it new from the man who merely makes it: the scavenger from the salvage expert. Creative design offers the artistic matron a choice of Op Art, Mondrian, or Matisse. If it exists, someone will make it new, or knock it off. We have this lust. It now leads us to feed on ourselves. Communications provide the means by which we are fed. We might ask what will be left of John Kennedy, the man, when the total electric drama of communications has finished with the legend. Questions concerning custody of the remains should not distract us from what is happening. The piranha fish of communications will settle this problem in transit. The old man of the sea will beach a skeleton, not a fish.

The appropriation of privacy is now accepted by those believed to still have it. We might think of Hemingway, and his ambiguous reluctance; of Picasso, and his too willing collaboration. Are we to assume their private lives are the last of their works? This once imperatively posthumous volume has now been moved up in the time schedule. Having exhausted the works, communications now insist on the man. While he is still with us: while he still has, that is, something further to exhaust.

In the case of Picasso it is commonly said that he has lived to experience his place in *history*. Instant fame bequeaths instant immortality. If this should prove to be so, our immortal lives will soon prove to be as brief, or briefer, than our mortal coils. The illusion of a stable, unchangeable past, into which we can escape from a mercurial, dissolving present, is symbolized in our mania for Halls of Fame, and the speed with which we populate them. They are already open-air mortuaries. Living men are draped with togas and hustled over to pose with the dead ones. It is felt that if a man can make it through the door, he is safe: that the winds of change blowing off the crematories will not so soon dispense with his ashes. Yet these mausoleums are no sooner up than they are crowded with forgotten immortals. The youth listens, mystified, to his father's panegyrics of Lindbergh, Red Grange, and possibly Jim Thorpe, as remote in time as Hector and Achilles. Momentarily the late show keeps alive the ghosts of Buster Keaton, Charlie Chaplin, Greta Garbo, Humphrey Bogart, Laurel and Hardy, but the calculated revival has little to do with "nostalgia." It is a way of warming up and serving food not yet removed from the cafeteria counter. Among Picasso's many gifts is his intuitive sense of what is "happening" — and what is happening, every hour on the hour, is the liquidation of reputations. A shrewd man, he may be willing to settle for "immortality" in his own time, sensing that the past, as well as the present, is now in the process of being liquidated.

Our current interest in the *present*, in all of its manifestations, resulting in the coffee-break art of the "happening," is less a true mystique of the here and now than a premature exhaustion of the familiar sources. If it is *new*, it has not yet been exhausted: if not exhausted, we accept it as new. This cultivates the panic that is felt by modern artists and promotes the quakes at the base of recent movements. A common mania obsesses these artists and the scientists of the space program. It can easily be capsuled: crack the barriers, or crack up. For the space-borne, there is the miracle of science: for the earthbound, the miracle of drugs. How right it is to describe it as a *Trip*. The object of both is to get into orbit and out of this world. This mystique is currently widespread and assumed to be remarkably modern. Those who form the priesthood promote it as *the* modern state of mind. The insights of both gifted and deranged men are used to encourage still further derangement. In this avant-garde establishment the luminous corpse is still Rimbaud's sacred disorder, a doctrine that gives the stamp of approval to any rebellious or perverse posture. The world is mad: so let the artist be madder than the world. We need not question that this insight once had a purpose, and served it. But to be madder than the world is neither fresh nor possible. Madmen are everywhere, in wearisome bounty, and exhaust this disorder as a land of promise. Madness we have had. Quite possibly the new thing is sanity. Behind the frequently theatrical façade of rebels who are now preoccupied with causes, I am struck by how remarkably sane their daydreams are. Far-fetched, it's true, but appallingly sane. They don't want stupid wars, they don't want to live stupid lives. The sheer novelty of it is not overwhelming, but the concept is still revolutionary. Not to wantonly kill, not to blight or destroy, not to live stupid lives.

Twenty years after a war that defies comprehension, a blight and destruction that defy calculation, those who experienced this disaster now feverishly prepare for the next one. Does it seem strange that the young express their noncomprehension in gestures rather than words? The four-letter placard is such a gesture. It is meant to be shock treatment for shock. The *absurd* hopefully serves the same purpose, but how do we define the absurd? Mr. Ronald Reagan is now a man of "presidential timber" and Governor of a state where Mrs. Gaye Spiegelman, mother of eight, is one of the celebrated topless entertainers. The absurd is what is commonplace. Absurdities constitute our daily quota of *what's new*.

The art of appropriation is so widely practiced its major accomplishments often go unnoticed. In appropriating we are merely doing what comes naturally. It is always done in the public's interest, with the public's will. Pinocchio and Cinderella now belong to Mr. Disney the way the Campbell's soup can belongs to Mr. Warhol. In this transformation Mr. Campbell and the tomato have disappeared. Whether it is Oedipus, Hamlet, or Huck Finn, the modern critic's task is appropriation. I think especially of Leslie Fiedler's remarkable repossession of Huck Finn. In making it new he surely made it his own. Neither the author nor the non-updated reader would suffer the shock of recognition.

As every modern schoolboy knows, however, the work of art does not belong to the author. It belongs to us all. The critics merely follow the dictates of modern practice. The most successful technique of critical appropriation is to reveal all that eluded the author. How little — it turns out — he knew his own mind. And if it did not elude the author it is safe to say it will not interest the critic. Revelation of this sort is the legitimate way to appropriate.

In this sense the work of art is but the raw material for an endless series of appropriations. Since we cannot fully fathom the artist's intent (a cardinal point of modern critical doctrine), it seems only sensible, as well as more creative, to impose our own. We call this, and rightly, making it our own. In this wise we have come to know the classic as the book too deep to know itself, and the artist as too complex to know himself. We know the critic as the man who holds the key. The element of value in this performance should not distract us from what is happening: we have the license to take what we want, do with it what we will. A satisfactory esthetic will soon follow on and enlighten this practice. We are all artists. Our raw material is art. It is a tribute to the depth and resources of art that it is not, as of this moment, exhausted, but around the diggings, like the entrance to mines, arise the huge slag heaps of interpretation. Diggers' permits are required for those who would like to tamper around.

The absurd theatre of war abroad, the absurd theatre of peace at home, make up the scene that provides us with our daily diet of communications. The right to pursuit of happiness is now being sought for the necrophiliac, open-air mortuaries where he can freely lie down with his love. The daily parody of commonplace life outstrips the invention of the satirist. We learn that life has the license to do what art has not. This provides the metaphysic of rebellion for those who seek a total freedom, and this freedom approximates how things really are. The lower depths, so long pastured in hell, have come up for a midsummer night's frolic. Crowding the turnstiles at the exits are the experts from all fields of communications, and a lawyer from the Civil Liberties Union. In the world of total freedom only the victim has lost his inalienable rights.

On the evidence, the cracking of barriers is no longer a national emergency. Such barriers as we once had are already down or scheduled for dismantling. What the rebel may now feel in the way of resistance is the predictable limits of human response. This may prove to be a barrier nothing will crack.

Principles of disorder once important to art, or to the cause of intellectual freedom, are now the clichés of a *derrière garde* who find the license of disorder profitable. In less than a decade the perverse, the criminal, and the psychotic have found acceptance as a standard for artistic integrity and achievement. We need not question that this looney bin has its function and even its museum of luminous corpses, but it now belongs in the sideshow wings of culture. We have had it. We live with it daily. It is no longer necessary for the artist to supply it. The demonism of this art is self-indulgent in the light of our proven capacity for evil, our daily torment of achieved savagery and impotent rage. What monster has not been seen and reported? What horror has not been committed and promoted? Is there a Prince of Darkness not out on bail or safe in the docket of the criminal's rights? Is there a crime still deprived of its victim, a perversity that has not been demonstrated? The evil men do is an open book, while the good men do is an unfashionable mystery. None of this is new but it is tiresome, and in the name of freedom falsifies experience. If strange things are now committed in the name of art, perhaps art must expand its commission. If we no longer know what art is, if the artist, indeed, refuses to make it, this must be the first of our acknowledgments that things are no longer as they seem, a keystone in our awareness of how they now are.

At the moment when the artist has never had it so good, museums without walls, a public without number, a theatre in the round and happenings in the square, art itself may prove to be expendable, a commodity that occupies a place in our wills, rather than our lives. At the moment when the writer never had it so good, his works available at the price of a sandwich, the sandwich may prove to be the public's better buy. The grapes of wrath cannot be eaten, Lady Chatterley cannot be loved. No bill of rites will silence or appease our hunger for more of the facts than we possess: no bill of goods supplies us with an illusion commensurate with our needs. The one frontier unexplored is our diminishing consciousness. Can we say that it has found a representative voice in the infectious double-talk of the younger generation, about to put to sea with Ringo in the Yellow Submarine? — perhaps the brightest exhibit in our expanding Museum of Happenings.

II: *The Leaning Tower of Pizza*

Question Man: What is a beatnik?

Answer by San Francisco Carpenter: Beatniks are happy people. They write poetry. Drink red mountain wine. A beautiful life. You can't find them. They're in hiding. Beatniks like to live in the country. If they must live in the city they work for the Post Office.

A happy people. A beautiful life. They carry the mail, they carry a tune, they carry the bug. Little wonder the virus is contagious, since happiness and love are its major symptoms. But the present epidemic has *spread*, rather than grown. It is a crabwise, horizontal movement that finds the perpendicular unsympathetic. Prophylactic measures applied to the beatnik (to control his anti-square behavior) have resulted in the new, resistant virus of the hippie. Some feed on the resistance: others are fed, like pigeons, by touring squares. If isolated, a member of the hippie culture is soon the center of a colony. No vaccine takes. The virus of the flower children spreads on wings of song. Simultaneous outbreaks of the disturbance have been noted in Palma, Casablanca, Copenhagen, West Orange, N.J., and Kyoto. Guards familiar with the type are now posted at the borders to curtail the spread of the affliction. They're no longer in hiding. You can find them wherever you look. They have their own casbahs in the cities and they are now colonizing the suburbs. For some time now we have been their neighbors, feeding their cats. Hippie cats, plain or fancy, lead the same voice-full, care-free lives. Our colony numbers, besides four cats, from five to a score of hippies. We like their non-fixed cats and they like our potato peeler fine.

It is rumored that you can't tell the boys from the girls, but that is unfounded. The boys are cuter. Some wash and coif. Some hum and strum. All adorn themselves. The male of the species dons the feathers the female sheds. In our colony some walk, some ride, some commute via Pan Am, some hitch on the freeway, some dig, some trip, and some peel potatoes. With our floating blade, patented peeler. They are not enemies of some progress. When they borrow the peeler my wife says, "Why don't you just keep it?" But they would not be beholden. There is more to the hippie than hurts the eye. There is the paradox. He has rejected the dry-cleaned uniform of the square for one that is not cleaned, but concealing. More is exposed, here and there, but less is revealed. The square has a face, of sorts. The hippie has a beard. In the square uniform, the individual is muted. In the beat-hippie uniform he is often liquidated. Of this and other ultimate questions I have wanted to speak with my neighbor, Luke. He says Hi to me when I go down for the mail. I say Hi to him. On my mailbox is what is left of my name and address after a winter of wind and cloudbursts. On his mailbox — a con-traption of wood, ornamented by hand with primary colors — is the legend

THE LEANING TOWER OF PIZZA

There is no number. The mail is sorted by the one who works for the P.O.

What do they do? They come and go. Mostly they seem to come. We share the drive, and the lights of their cars ripple on our exposed beam ceiling. Lower down there is also some smoke from their exhausts. My wife says, "Here they come!" and we both adjust our sleep belts. I lie on my side, staring at the clock. I see it slantwise, elliptic, like a nebula spiraling. I tilt it upright, say, "Twenty past three," or "Ten past four." They are nightowls, occasionally hootowls, but usually silent on arrival. They come like Orientals crossing a border on padded cat feet, dope and weed laden. I lie thinking of Chinatown opium smugglers with their hands in their sleeves. Later, there may be a shot of music and the green light of dawn on the unwashed windows. It's the dawn that cools it. We loosen our belts and go back to sleep.

Much later, toward noon, I watch two girls and a boy (he has the beard) each with a blanket roll, a rucksack, crotch-tight Levis and tire-soled huaraches, take off for Muir Woods, a festival in Monterey, a week in Mendocino, or a preach-in at Berkeley. Southbound travelers will carry a placard with the letters L.A. on it. They have learned about placards. They are masters of the two, three, and four-letter sign.

Still later, as I stand sprinkling the fuchsias, a random flock in bizarre and exotic plumage, like children dressed for a Halloween party, make their way serenely past me in skirts that drag, with trains that trail, or neither trail nor drag but bind above the knees, minimum-skirt style, or in low-rise pants on a high-rise swingster, in hats that spread and glow like lampshades, or astronautically perk. They are off for a swinging time wherever the action is. I go with them, afoot and light-headed, to the end of the drive.

A hard day's night later, with the hoodlum in the Jeep who throws the morning paper like a Molotov cocktail, they are back, the lights ripple on the ceiling, and my wife turns to say, "Here they come!" I think of the redcoats. I think of night-riding Paul Revere. I also think of the Volkswagen bus parked in the lot behind the supermarket, its windows painted black and a legend on the windshield —

DON'T LAUGH. YOUR DAUGHTER MAY BE INSIDE.

My friend Luke is the bridge between his own kind and the rest of us squares. He is a sable toward auburn-haired mature-type hippie, with a gold-flecked, reddish, D. H. Lawrence-type beard, good teeth, shy eyes, and capable almost square-type hands. In the lobe of one ear he wears a thin gold ring of the type worn by muchachas south of the border. I don't know about the other. His sable-toned mane sweeps low on the right side, and he seems to feel his left side is for squares. His manner is gentle. His voice is so low I receive more media than message.

For relaxing, reflecting, or gabbing with squares, Luke wears frayed levis, GI infantry boots, and a UCLA sweatshirt. In full regalia, headed for the action, he wears a wide-wale, hip-length, fawn-colored jacket, a four-in-hand kerchief, stirrup heel boots with green and gold stitching, an eight gallon size sombrero with rattlesnake band bought on safari in Chihuahua. The effect is that of Lawrence in Taos, passing as Buffalo Bill. I have found Luke intelligent, cultivated, informed, and sensitive to the problems of squares. After a harder day's night than usual I left a brief note in the hand-crafted mailbox. It was tactfully wrought to suggest that a good night's sleep was also part of the beautiful life.

Days later I found my answer. It may have been there for some time. It was placed in the path at the side of the house where I spend much time sprinkling fuchsias, half concealed by the gravel that held it in place. I felt the shock of recognition that secretly binds even hippies and squares.

In a round, legible hand Luke regretted the disturbance and agreed with my opinion on the importance of sleep. As for the cause of the annoyance, he commented in passing — "Youth is groovy. So much energy and inspiration, but I imagine it makes it difficult to live in close proximity to."

So I had not misjudged him. *Close proximity to* is hard to beat. Youth *is* groovy; both the one he has and lives, and the one that I, sprinkling fuchsias, remember. It seemed to me that things were looking up for hippies and squares. The moment was at hand for me to put to Luke something in the way of ultimate questions. Is it all a beautiful, happy life, or is some of it a drag? Did he prefer selling stamps or delivering the mail for the local P.O.? I wanted to put to him the sixty-four-dollar question: Didn't the hippie conceal as much as he revealed? Was that his intention? What were the facts behind the façade?

That was some time ago. Just recently, what was concealed about Luke was revealed. I was standing in the gravel path, sprinkling the fuchsias, as he took off on safari. He didn't say Hi. I could hear the slap of his beat-bare feet. My view was somewhat concealed by a bush of camellias, but there was no mistaking the hat. He never fails to wear it when he is headed for the action. Otherwise, however, he wore not a stitch, and his sable-toned hair is shorter than Lady Godiva's. Not a boot, not a sock, not a fly-snagged zipper, not a T-shirt, a sweatshirt, or a mini-kini. Like Adam he was, and made his way with bold confidence toward Eden.

Down a street lined with houses, matrons at their chores, small fry at their ruin, outlaws arriving, in-laws departing, Luke made his way to where small children played in the silvery arc of a sprinkler. The water appealed. As reported by a stupefied witness he cried aloud, "Water! Water!" like the Ancient Mariner. The children disappeared. He relaxed, bathed, cooled himself. Refreshed, he then made his way in the direction of the firehouse where he was met by the resources of a paralyzed culture, firemen, tired men, delinquents, loafers, and the long arm of the law. I have it all by hearsay, being, as we say, lost in thought.

Later I learned that Luke, having taken a trip, then left to recover his familiar surroundings, had put on his hat and taken off for where the action is. He found it. Currently out on bail, he is back in the leaning tower of Pizza, where, as I lie there brooding, the amber nightlight burns.

Is it a new or an old dream of the good life? None other is both current and selling. Neither language nor culture has proved to be a barrier. Neither poverty, affluence, nor influence matter. Youth is groovy. Life is lovely, and there are flowers for its adornment. There are also some pretty good people behind it — if you look far enough. If you dig the lonely bit there is Walden Pond, where you can shack up with your genius. If you dig the social bit you can take to the road, to the beach, or to the leaning tower of Pizza. If you dig social rights you can practice civil rites and disavow civil wrongs. The open road is the parabola of the picket line. Just a century ago another poet put it like this —

> This then is the life
> Here is what has come to the surface after so many
>   throes and convulsions
> How curious! How real!
> Underfoot the divine soil, overhead the sun.

Starting from Paumonok, North Beach, Des Moines, Waukegan, Wagon Wheel, Prairie Sac, Ogallala, bearded and sauntering, afoot and lighthearted, done with bitching, whimpering, grudging, and shrugging, Walt Whitman, that cosmos, leads the way down the long asphalt path, the still almost open road. He too fits the picture. He believes in happy people. He leads the beautiful life. Solitary, singing in the West, he strikes up for the beautiful life.

What is commonest, cheapest, nearest, easiest, is ME,
Me going in for my chances, spending for vast returns,
Adorning myself to bestow myself on the first that will
    take me.

The hippie on the corner, in the country, in hiding, in the classroom, the men's room, the campus cafeteria where he sits stirring coffee with a tongue depresser, never had it so common, so cheap, so near, and with so many takers of his adornment. It's a beautiful life. You can say that again: it's a beautiful life. The style is the man, and the man is his own work of art. He sings, celebrates, and dresses himself. The home-spun suit, the shirt open at the throat, the good gray beard, the soft broadbrim hat, the fraternal, affectionate, beguiling gaze, Walt Whitman was there firstest, and there with the mostest. The mystique of the tramp, the brotherhood of the open road, the fraternity of the free, buffeting winds of heaven, the beat-hippie inherits the life the good gray poet promised.

I tramp a perpetual journey, (come listen all!)
My signs are a rain-proof coat, good shoes, and a staff
    from the woods,
No friend of mine takes his ease in my chair,
I have no chair, no church, no philosophy,
I lead no man to a dinner-table, library, exchange . . .

Is it the media or the message? No chairs, no churches, no tables, no libraries — just a few sleeping bags, paperbacks, and fruitboxes. What was once a modest seller under the counter is now the best-seller over the counter. Not Whitman's barbaric yawp over the roofs of the world, but the grass, the fix, and the overnight lie-in. Youth is groovy: one hundred years had to pass before they got Walt's pitch in the new translation. Something new, and cool; the bumper strip reads

KEEP CALIFORNIA GREEN WITH GRASS!

One hundred long years had to pass before the message was distinguished from the media.

I loafe and invite my soul
I lean and loafe at my ease observing a spear of summer
    grass.

So far so good — but *this* good, gray-bearded beat poet goes on too long, and works too hard at it. There is too much perspiration in it. For all his loafing at his ease, for all his digging the grass, for all his talk about the sunshine, the moonshine, the lovers, the perpetual journey Whitman tramps has the smell of the inkstand and the nightlamp. For all his talk about fraternity, the old man is a loner. For all his praise of the idler, he is a worker, a craftsman who calculates the smallest effect. The saunterer's loitering, the loafer's gossiping, the grass stains on the shoes, the knees, and the elbows, do not conceal that when the Muse calls him this idler will report for work. To that extent he is a square manqué. The rain-proof coat, good shoes, and staff from the woods he puts behind the door while he punches the time clock.

From *Leaves of Grass* to *Howl*, from Whitman to Ginsberg, is the downhill fight of the perpetual tramp. That archetype square, Horatio Alger, had to grow up, fold up, and then dry up. He had to tramp the perpetual journey in reverse. Alger's Ragged Dick and Tattered Tom are still with us, however, bigger than life, at the Hollywood Palace; after a hard day's night they are up there with Ed Sullivan. The way to fight City Hall is to sit or lie in it, the way to fight poverty is live in it, the way to rise above it is to cool it, the way to get with it is to smoke it, and the way to really take it with you is to take the *trip*. "When in doubt, turn off your mind, relax, float downstream." This word of guidance from the new Tao, *The Psychedelic Experience*, will serve as obit to that *ur-mensch* Horatio Alger. The new guru, Dr. Timothy Leary, also has some advice on the art of seduction.

Under marijuana, with your senses heightened, you're not going to go to bed with a crude seducer. It's not seduction at all. It's a highly intricate, delicate, exquisite enhancer of communication. If you have an alcoholic man coming on to a girl who is smoking marijuana, nothing's going to happen except the horrified shrinking back on the part of the marijuana smoker.

But what is going to happen if the marijuana hippie is coming on to the alcoholic girl? Something's going to happen more than horrified shrinking. Something both old and new in the line of communications. So much depends on the girl in proximity to.

Youth is groovy. Luke has said so. It's many things to many people but it's not eternal. You can't put it in your pipe and smoke it. I would like to ask Luke, as we say, what arrangements he has made for the eventualities. What is done with *old* beats? Are they retooled and repainted or liquidated? Is there a sure-fire dirt-ring dating method? If there isn't, how do you tell? The bearded traffic on the highway is heavy, and I sometimes see the spit and image of Albert Schweitzer. He walks with a staff. He might be father time. From the potato peeler borrower my wife has learned his B average in Math keeps him out of the draft. He is twenty-three. He is thinking of the Peace Corps if things get worse. Is there a secret hippie way to hang on without growing old? To my knowledge, hippie life and thought have not had much to say on this subject. Or on dying. No, they are all for coming on strong. Their songs and stories are silent on the subject of Forest Lawn. I've not been asked, but I visualize a greensward sloping to the sea, tipped for the sun's bask, with nothing more than the beard-combed grass. Here and there lint from the blankets, the weapon-shaped depression of a sleeping bag. In the pits of marijuana ash the shards of dreams, still cooling. No place for scoffers. Close proximity to the last!

Watching them come and go, I wonder about those who have come and gone. I'd rather not broach the subject to Luke. Are old hippies put back in circulation as middle-aged squares? Having served their time, like the chaps at San Quentin, are they given a suit of clothes, pocket money, and obliged to shift and make time for themselves? Worse than death? A slipping hippie might think so. It might be why I see so little of him. Does he slink off to a place in the woods, like cats do, and curl up to die with his guitar? Or does he just slink off and turn up snarling on a used car lot? There is no part-time good place, no Between-the-Acts for old hippies. Youth is groovy, life is lovely, and you've solved the marijuana seduction problem, or there's one seducer less in the leaning tower of pizza. Is he listed as missing in action, or *inac-*

tion? Or does he just fade away like old generals. I mean to ask Luke.

Almost as pressing as the old-hippie problem is the new dilemma of rags to riches. Or rather rags *and* riches. Some have no choice. Poverty to the swinging, strumming hippie has got to be a luxury item. The hippie who makes the scene can no longer afford it. Fame and fortune hammer his pad door daily. Hollywood beckons. Ed Sullivan calls. A hard day's night means *bread,* baby, and it can't be helped.

And too much bread means the new *kitsch* hippie of Carnaby styling and high Mod fashion. He left London this morning. He comes padding up the drive with a blue flight bag. This affluent perversion of *echt* hippie ethic has caught on where things have to catch, among the young. "Sherpa"-lined vests, "Granny" shirts, wide-wale corduroy, houndstooth checks, military-type jackets with World War I tunics, vinyl caps, Norfolk jackets, suede shoes and stirrup heel boots, the ensemble available at a price that would keep the leaning tower in pizzas for months. The *echt* family of hippies, starved as saltimbanques, with their harlequin children in a Goodwill perambulator, turn to gaze with the shocked indignation of squares at the upstart Mods snorting by in their Fiats, their long coiffed hair blowing and their Fat Max ties puffing like sails. What are the hippies coming to? The old American pay-off: success. You start with something *echt,* and the *kitsch* takes over. You deliver the mail and the Mods collect it. They loaf around on the corners, they walk along the highways, they fill up the classrooms, they scent up the washrooms, they heat up the cool scene, they louse up the good scenes, they jam up the ways and the means to the action, and one fine day the lights of their cars will ripple on the exposed beams of our ceilings.

My wife will say, "Here they come!" and there they will be. We will tighten our sleep belts and wait for the leaning tower to fall.

A more insidious threat to hippie ethic is underground creative backsliding. The intellectual hippie is subject to weaving, carving, painting, strumming, performing, composing, even thinking. Not for long, and seldom for good, but it links him to the treadmill of effort, the jackpot, and the pay-off. He has rejected things, but not the nature of things. Many bear the seal of Good American Living and Housekeeping. In his reluctance toward self-improvement — when that is all that is left him — he confronts the ultimate issues so deftly sidestepped by Walt Whitman. To improve is to corrupt: even love takes some effort. Seduction is sicklied o'er with perspiration. It comes naturally, but it takes some doing, nevertheless. The good hippie wants to be, rather than become: he wants a role rather than a goal. The perpetual journey is a raft floating downstream. Hints of mysterious doctrine, East and West, occupy the honored place in his fruitboxes. Madame Blavatsky speaks to him, although at too great a length. So do the masters of Zen, *Lord of the Flies,* Joan Baez, Bob Dylan, and The Grateful Dead. He derives from this exposure a state of mind not unlike the charms of marijuana. Understandably, marijuana is more popular. The weed, the fix, and the trip appropriate the experience without the labor involved in its acquirement, the travel that both uplifts and broadens is five dollars the trip. The widening of horizons, the expansion of the soul, the elevation and refinement of sensation, is a spectacle that takes place behind the balls of the eye, not before them. The theatre is interior. Poets have always known it, squares have always feared it. But the square can no longer obstruct what is nothing so much as the march of his progress, the pill that frees him from pain and labor, the fix that minimizes the role of will. The oral contraceptive dispenses with risk, and LSD dispenses with effort. When in doubt — and who is not in doubt? — turn off your mind.

Along with Marshall McLuhan, the vanishing beatnik anticipated the imminent liquidation of the Gutenberg Mythos, the power of the written word. It was at this juncture that the beat rebellion and the Dodge rebellion joined forces. The *literate* person had proved to be expendable. Literacy had become the media of his corruption. The paradox of the beat rebellion was that it was housed and fed on the college campus, the mausoleum and deep-freeze of the square's inexhaustible nostalgia. The library was his Shelter, his commissary the cafeteria, his life of the mind the seminar and the classroom. His Bill of Rights got their hearing, and he could walk or run to the nearest sit-in, relax in the lie-in, and carry the placards at the preach-in. At this Platonic banquet, rubbing elbows with the squares, the beatnik-hippie rebel achieved a nonliterate breakthrough, the rediscovery and ploy of the four-letter word.

With the appearance of the hallucinogenic drugs the relatively active beat has become the inactive hippie: the committed beat becomes the noncommitted hippie. A predictable yearning for Eastern wisdom is combined with an urgent need for psychedelic expansion. Disenchantment with squares motivates some of the recruits, but what of those who have never experienced enchantment? *Disen-chantment comes later.* (There will be no enchantment until the euphoria of the drug experience.) In the main it is a sentiment exported from the world of squares. Numberless squares share it. It is square disenchantment that generates the power that keeps the lights of the scene burning. The envy of squares warms and pumps the hippie heart. It is why, with his love of Nature, Indians, sleeping bags, and hand-ground acorn flour, he colonizes the city ghetto in preference to life in the woods. In the woods he is alone, with Hiawatha. In Haight-Ashbury he is at home with the tribe. The woods are also lacking in the glowing heartburn of the squares.

Disenchanted squares, or those deprived of their childhood, identify with the scene and serve as its promoters. The more literary become its apologists. To a greater length and degree than the hippies themselves, they explain and promote the "happening" for outsiders. The curious hippie reads more about his condition than he writes. Perhaps he hears more about it than he knows. He looks into the eyes of squares for his current Nielsen rating. Newspapers and magazines daily provide him with an *apologia pro vita sua*. To a substantial degree this may have retarded the emergence of gifted and qualified spokesmen. There is a quantity of rainmaking song and dance, a minimum of sense.

For the acid head, both sense and enchantment are part of the "trip." But in the troughs of these waves of enlightenment his karma is a form of fatigue. It might easily be confused with the clichés of noninvolvement, or the serene disengagements of the swami or guru. Lacking all motive the hippie stasis resembles peace. Such a posture is new to the American scene but is a natural by-product of the machinery of culture. The spectacle of this machinery in perpetual motion is more than sufficient to produce the fatigue symptoms. The child who will not eat, who sits without appetite at a table groaning with American bounty, suffers from a similar revulsion and subconscious refusal to participate. The very abundance of the scene repels it. The clichés still viable for both young and old squares — the pep literature on the cereal boxes — reduce rather than encourage appetite. So many breakfasts of so many champions produce the first dropout. He doesn't want to eat: worse, he refuses to play. The games grown-ups play, the rat-races they run, the frenzied whirring spectacle of the culture in motion, although stimulating to the addicted square, stupefy the uninitiated. To recoil from this experience is a simple gesture of survival. The first and last rejection is *education,* the learning process itself. Where does it lead but to death in the labyrinth? The winding approaches to the modern freeway parallel this indoctrination. The mechanical roar, the sluicing lanes of traffic, the blighted wastelands of hell visible through the fences, are appropriate symbols for the nature of this passage. There is no turning back. A moving finger of neon writes —

YOU WHO ENTER HERE

ABANDON ALL HOPE

Sound advice. And the sentiment is commonplace. It is in the wife's parting kiss at the kitchen door. One leaves the relative sanity of the house to participate in the machinery of culture, with the leisure world asylum or the coronary at the end of the run. The savage parable of the scene itself dispenses with the need of commentary. In these lanes the roaring cars, the whining sirens, the druglike flow toward the unmentionable climax: in those across the way, mile upon mile of stationary bugs, each concealing a time bomb of seething, impotent rage. A single fuse smokes from exhaust to exhaust: but nothing goes off. To what avail the disciplines, the long postponements, the data stored away in the mind's bomb shelter? To what noble, fruitful purpose the privileged years of schooling? The senior citizen who now plods back for more of it —

what does he do but pass a final judgment on it? Can life have taught him so little — and can there be so little left to his life? The old folks who now inspire the adult education program subtly undermine the program that produces such adults. If they had actually *lived* a life, would they now yearn, like children, to go back to school? In their very desire to make up for lost time, the time they seek to regain has been devalued. The dropout can only ask, what *good* is something that has done so little good? In the swelling ranks of adult education we have the key to the swelling ranks of dropouts. The *scene* is not made in the pages of the Harvard Classics, or the One Hundred Great Books.

Hippie-style it is currently being made in the public-private haunts of the flower children. No one knows their number. Computers only tell us what they will or won't buy. Hippie-kinship to the classical or amateur bohemian is more deceptive than instructive. Its essential use is that of a label for baffled squares. The Haight-Ashbury scene has commitment and style, an ethic of love, freedom, and fraternity, but on the evidence it is sadly lacking in brains. The disciplines crucial to rudimentary thought are unfortunately alien to the hippie psyche. They involve work. That entails effort. Both will easily prove to be a strain. Hippies share some knowledge of where they have been, but no demonstrable insight into where they are going. This too is as it should be. What they share is a condition, not a direction. The condition is that of adolescent rebellion, a stage in the normal development of the species. Regardless of the number of the participants it will not likely develop into a movement. How the hippie acts is a matter of how he feels: he alternately feels like tuning in and dropping out. This simple and essential fact of nature determines the nature of the hippie situation, a scene congenial to all who share the condition of growing up. They have each other. There are times when this is more than enough. In their dreams they fulfill, rather than begin, their responsibilities.

If we think of leaning towers, it is sometimes hard to tell which tower is leaning,* the hippie's or the square's. An impartial observer might find that one tower inclines forward in the morning, the other backward in the evening. The inhabitants of both towers often smoke the same pipe dreams and come on to the same girl without enough marijuana. In the morning, light or heavy-footed, they both tramp the same perpetual journey, but it's a fact that the square will end up with the sorer feet. His perpetual journey is perhaps more perpetual.

The hippie ethos is tribal, and reflects his rejection of the demands and the rewards of individual effort. But his withdrawal without pain from the pains of the world has a long and respectable history. His adolescent rejection of the world does not reject the world of the adolescent. Hand in hand, with wandering steps and slow, they haunt the lost suburbia of Eden, or loaf at their ease in the grassy Groves of Academe. If they have nothing but each other, it still puts them one up on those who have all the rest. The Jefferson Airplane will whizz them into orbit, and The Grateful Dead will comfort them in heaven.

> We live a life of ease
> Everyone of us has all we need
> Sky of blue and sea of green
> In our Yellow Submarine.

* Late reports (fall of '67) indicate the Leaning Tower of Pizza is falling, the inhabitants dispersing. The speed with which this scene "emerged" and now declines, is an example of the instant appropriation, exploitation, and liquidation of the news media. The hippie is still with us. It is the *media* that has spent itself.

To the captive square this has the *ur*-appeal of the noble or ignoble savage, the child of nature, the free, pre-civilized man. Some will feel toward him the longing of a paradise lost, others a paradise regained. In the currently deflated coin of the realm the hippie sings and loves for his supper, smiling tunefully down from the pizza heights of his leaning tower.

III: *Mom & Pop Art*

The Leisure World of Objets d'Art

I loved her in a dress she wore in the first
ambush scene, and I loved the sweater and
skirt she's wearing when they're sharing up
the money. JERRY SCHATZBERG
of *Bonnie and Clyde*

The classic Pop Art tableau in America is the
White House and its inhabitants, Poppabird, Ladybird,
Lyndabird, and the beagle with ears for handles. Next in
status and coverage is Senator Everett Dirksen as a guest
and performer on the Red Skelton show, leading the TV
audience in a sonorous pledge to the flag. These tableaus
surpass, in a way not to be overtaken, the ambitious crea-
tions of the serious Pop artist, and the bounds of his art.
What more can be done with this material? The medium
bogs. Comment can go no farther than the scene itself,
nor hope to reach an audience of such numberless millions. The Pop *image* is itself a work of Pop Art.

In this confrontation the aspiring Pop artist finds himself in a common *communications* problem. All artists
share it. How speak louder, or clearer, or truer, than the
thing itself? The revelatory subject defies commentary. It

speaks inexhaustibly. It also speaks on prime time. It is a matter of time — and that would be prime time — before the stars with top billing on Capitol Hill say a word between the acts for General Motors, safe in the knowledge that what is good for one is good for all of us. Ex-Presidents might put in a dignified word for golf or, if not active sportsmen, for Missouri Meerschaum corncob pipes. If the auspices of such a program are elevated — Alcoa, Xerox, or Hallmark Cards — the performance itself would be considered acceptable. Already stars of stage, screen, and the headlines lend their faces and voices to the TV commercial — and the commercial, in turn, supplies stage and screen with some of its stars. This week's charming airline hostess may be next week's heroine in *Gunsmoke*. Why not? It is often difficult to distinguish between the dramas and the commercials. More time and talent, obviously, often go into the ads.

The phenomenon of taste, the subsoil of manners, has not merely shifted on the lower levels, but abandoned those positions that were once assumed to be higher. How to behave? Very few citizens seem to know. A mother of eight develops her talents as a topless dancer. A distinguished public figure entertains Red Skelton's fans with a reading of the prayer "Man is Not Alone," found on John Kennedy's desk. What is the case but magnificent for pitiless ferocity? So it has been long in coming. We have no reason to be surprised. When in doubt — and who is not in doubt? — we do what pays.

Although a long time maturing, the seeds of Pop Art have been found in local soil samples for decades. The man who put us all on the cover of the *Post* was our first and most cherished Pop artist. His living works of art still inhabit the suburbs, walk the streets, and run the country. We bear his stamp, just as his works bear ours.

If a problem exists in the production of Pop Art it lies in the role of the ready-made object, the objets d'art that can reproduce themselves. It's an old dilemma. Mr. Andy Warhol merely points it up. The question is no longer *What is Pop Art* — but what is not. Too many ready-made objects can't seem to help turning up as art. A further complication lies in advertising and the emergence of the *Image:* are the objets d'art in the label, or in the soup? The metaphysics of this problem cast a shadow on Ladybird's Keep America Beautiful Program. Which America? The one on the signboard or the one in the can? The curtailment of outdoor advertising *could* be a curtailment of art. It would leave us with the indoor variety only, or the outdoor stuff long stamped on the eyeballs. Pop Art is already a part of our nature, indoors or out. The outdoor variety is just a tiresome reminder of the art that hangs on the walls of the mind. When I see *tires* I still read Fiske. I see the boy in his "sleepers," like the pair I was wearing, yawning as he holds up both the tire and the candle, and I see the legend *Time To Retire* bright as luminous paint. After more than forty years I see the Mail Pouch sign on the roof of the barn. Nor do I really have to see it to taste the *chaw* or start the real Mail Pouch juices flowing. Just the roof of the barn, with the shingles warping, and what is left of the paint peeling, works so well for me I've never been obliged to buy or chew Mail Pouch to taste it. That's the lasting power and flavor of *echt* Pop Art.

Sometime before Marcel Duchamp recognized the latrine as a ready-made object of art, millions of Americans felt for ready-made objects a special appreciation. They were not merely useful. They proved to be miraculous. It was part of their remarkable nature to naturally reproduce themselves.

Long before the eggheads' museum without walls, the

grass-root hick and the plain dirt farmer had a free and current museum of ready-made objects. It offered him a prodigal choice. My copy of Sears, Roebuck, 1924, features a hand-painted picture of a great port on its cover. A steamship, a locomotive, a tug, and many factories puff pillars of smoke high as the towers of the city. Men and trucks are at work. Through the clouds of smoke and steam the towers of Zenith aspire above the morning mist. I gazed at it as a boy and I gaze at it now with a mindless, bottomless, longing. It is a bad painting but the artist who made it knew that I would paint in whatever proved to be missing. The colors were mine. I could fill in or brighten up what he had left out. Before I opened the door of this museum I was hopelessly sold on its contents. I was more than sold. I wanted to dream with it, privately. This sentiment was so commonplace and necessary a place had been found to indulge it. The catalogue, Sears or Monkey Ward, was one of the ornaments of privacy. It shared, with the dreamer, the cobwebbed seclusion of the privy, the monastic cell of the Protestant Pilgrim. Corked on one of the holes, like a stove lid, the book of promise open where the sunlight warmed it, as a boy I wandered, afoot and lighthearted, in the inexhaustible world of objects. Spring wind trains and stem wind watches, shadowy horses in gleaming black harness, buxom ladies in corsets, player pianos, harmonicas, drum sets, and ocarinas; 1000-shot airguns, double-barrel shotguns, cattlemen's jackknives, gentlemen's pearl knives, hunters, woodsmen, and Boy Scout knives; chain-tread bike tires, auto-seat buggies, russet leather saddles and cream separators, Magnavox speakers, superheterodyne receivers, water wings, boxing gloves, Louisville sluggers, pearl-handled razors, double swing strops, water pistols, Ouija boards, onyx marbles; shoes of pearl-leather uppers, green chrome leather soles, with chocolate-colored ankle and toe patches; watches with fobs, watches with chains, watches with snap-lid cases, open faces, twenty-three jewels and five adjustments, screw bezel, solid back, guaranteed not to turn the color of a doorknob or my money back. At least one of these things I might have had if I hand-shelled ten or twelve bushels of popcorn at twenty cents a bushel and didn't spend the money or lose it.

Did all this grandeur perish? Or does this leisure world of mail order objects, in living color and as near as your telephone, still paper the walls of the all-American mind? The latest Fall & Winter catalogue from Wards features more than fifteen hundred pages of goodies. That's up five hundred pages from what they once offered me.

A woman with seven children, a missing common-law husband, her food and her rent supplied by welfare, when asked in what way she felt the most deprived, replied, "What I feel the most deprived of is *things*. I'd like some more *things*."

Things occupy houses, inhabit rooms, jam stores and windows, have their own hiding places, have their leisure world, have their own retirement plans and insurance, have their own security, their own graveyards, and like good Americans, they have their own second chance to make a new start. Just north of San Francisco a sign reads —

WE BUY JUNK

AND

SELL ANTIQUES

Not only a life of their own, but a new life.

The home-spun cloth, the home-made chair, the home-canned fruit, the home-cooked meal, still have something to recommend them but they lack the crucial component:

newness. They are *old* things. They lead the life of the second-chance. The real things are new and ready-made. To know this is to be part of the leisure world of objects: to understand that the object is the model, not the thing itself. The value and uniqueness of the model is in its boundless self-reproduction: in its ready-madeness. This miracle was so commonplace it went unobserved until "discovered" by the Pop artist. These things are objets d'art Pop.

The predictable exhaustion of hand-made objects — most of them hand-soiled by the toil of the maker — turned the artist to the new, ever-expanding world of objects. For years he had felt them pressing in on him, for years he had foolishly made war on them. Then his eyes were opened. He saw them as the real things of this world. If you can't beat them, join them; if you join them you will find art wherever you look, real Pop Art. *Any* object or thing might qualify, might prove to be expressive, compulsive, or obsessive, but one class of objects beyond all others prove to be objects of art. Advertised objects. Objects with an *image*. Objects that are hard to distinguish from the *image*. Flags, soup cans, movie stars, supermen, or most of those things you find in the attic, if you still have one. There is a sure-fire test. If you don't miss it, but can't throw it out, it is Mom & Pop Art.

The unsung artists of our past, those who have shaped our lives more profoundly than we can imagine, are the anonymous creators of can and bottle labels, the illustrators of the mail order world of objects. What would the man who designed the Campbell's soup label think when he saw it in an art museum, or noted the price that such labels can bring, blown up on canvas, on the open market? Long before he had entered a museum, the American farmer had a museum of his own. The catalogue served him for art, literature, and instruction. In its last, tattered stages it occupied the privy. Each year's old promise was replaced with a dream that was new. In the privacy of his home, by lamplight, he could spend the long winter evenings just browsing. With a pencil, on the order blanks provided, he could make the elementary steps of acquisition, experience the torment and doubt of decision, be sensible, be practical, be long or short-sighted, brood on it for weeks, forget it, or mail it off and live in waiting. My father and I lived in waiting. He used red-capped indelible pencils that poked holes where he made decimal points and left a purple smear on the heel of his hand. In the sense important to the rise of Pop Art, the period of waiting was crucial. While living in waiting my father and I would often reflect back on our decisions. One watch came with a fob stamped with a locomotive, the one I ordered with a compass in the stem wind. It is the one that I didn't order that sticks in my mind. I looked at it most of the time during the period of waiting, and then I looked at it again when the other watch arrived. I consider this the germinal, seminal period of great Pop Art. Not objects, but the stand-ins for objects: in the life of the mind the stand-in was more important than the thing itself.

At this point the leisure world of objects had not yet emerged as objets d'art. A few aroused a longing, a distance of enchantment similar to priceless museum objects, but these were different to the extent that they had a price. They were still merely the desirable things of this world. In the cities, in the aisles of the emporiums, the browser could actually see and touch them, a pleasure forbidden to the browser in the museums. The sensible, discriminating woman soon distinguished between the idle, cultural trip to the museum, and the meaningful, gratifying venture to the bazaar. In the crowded aisles of the great emporiums the shopper is both a critic and a collector. The lower levels of taste are exercised and improved at the jousting around the bargain counters: the upper levels of taste are cultivated before the tableaus in the avenue windows. No art museum can approach such audience participation. No object of art will excite such admiration, appraisal, and scrutiny. It need hardly be added that the art of window dressing set the standards smart museums soon followed. This proved to be reciprocal, however, since the windows are dressed with museum objects. The shopper can't afford a Mondrian, or a Matisse, but she can afford a dress that *knocks them off*, a remarkably apt phrase. They are knocked off the pedestal appropriate to art, and made available to the public. Plagiarism is the exercise of acquisitive taste. The modern artists themselves have set the precedent in this fashion of appropriation. What they could use, wherever they found it, they took. Primitive masks are "made new" by Picasso, primitive scenes and customs by Gauguin. The esthetic of appropriation seems to lie in audacity. If done with style, and promoted with success, this sort of piracy is recognized as talent. There is one word of caution. *Make it new* refers to the label only — not the soup.

The contents of Pop Art will change daily — like display cases or what is new in advertising — but the principle behind it is the art and science of appropriation. What begins as Pop we appropriate as art. Pop comprehends what goes: it is how we think things are. With a Pop artist's license we can take the object with us, make it our own, offer it for resale. As art, every ready-made object is in the public domain. Many private bathrooms reflect this dilemma and resemble art galleries rather than bathrooms. Van Gogh or Picasso hang on the wall: the tub, the stool, and the bowl are ready-made sculptures. The alert Pop artist, an overnight guest, need only sign the object to appropriate it. If the signature is good it is a tub no longer, but an objet d'art. Such objects have a meaning beyond their function and are open to endless interpretations. An American dream is the throw-away salvaged as a work of art.

It would seem that we have always known, in our fashion, that everyday things would one day prove to be sacred. Time is redeemed in the attic, the salvage shop, and the lost and found department. Our escape from this surround of objects is in the miracle of their transformation. The Pop work of art comprehends the fetish object and the release, in laughter, of the obsession. Seeing it for what it *is*, we can laugh. All these years it has obscurely papered the walls of the mind. Release comes easily from the *image*, but we are not so easily freed from the objects. Some come without labels. Worse, some come without ads. This brings complexity to a movement primarily concerned with *things*, some to be transformed, some to be transfixed, some to be exorcised.

The poets and painters of advertising have refashioned the home into a museum of objects emblematic of the fantasies, rather than the lives, of the inhabitants. The goal of advertising is to dissolve the distinction between ready-made fantasy and life. Nothing touched, tasted, smoked, or smelled need be what it is. Separate togetherness is consummated with eye-shades, earplugs, the mini-TV, and the king-size beds. From a museum of her own, with fantasies of her own, the daughter of the house steps out of her frame to participate in the year-round self-celebrations and beauty pageants, where she will walk, talk, and smile like a living work of art. These exhibitions provide the gallery setting for the ready-made dolls created by advertising. The hair, the eyes, the teeth, the smile show the unmistakable hand of the potter: the object is unmistakably a work of Pop Art. The citation will read that "She had always been interested in art, in boys, in acting, in promoting peace, and looking as lovely as possible." This performance will be witnessed by an assemblage of parents, senior citizens, and beauty dropouts, for whom it is of more crucial importance than the participants. It is the word made flesh, the dream of life seen precisely as advertised. Mother may paint on the side, or practice Civil Rites, or promote World Peace, or merely master French cooking, but her lifelike baby doll is her real work of art.

Mr. Timm Ulrich, a Berlin artist, recently exhibited himself as a "perfect living total work of art." Would Mr. Ulrich recognize that Miss Teenage America had done him one better? She needs no cage. She needs no slogan. Art is life, and in *her* life it is art. She needs to demonstrate nothing, state or manifest nothing, or proclaim to be more than anyone can see she is — a living work of art. As a small concession, to put an end to rumors and to stress the word *living,* she has agreed to dress, undress, take steps, talk, and even sing. In these living dolls the leisure world of objects achieves the ultimate in Pop Art, and Mom & Pop take their rightful place in our Halls of Fame.

IV: *Children Are the Best People*

> Actually the Child is in many ways the most valuable part of the personality, and can contribute to the individual's life exactly what an actual child can contribute to family life: charm, pleasure and creativity. If the Child in the individual is confused and unhealthy, then the consequences may be unfortunate, but something can and should be done about it.   DR. ERIC BERNE

For how long, unstated but implicit, have we believed that children are the best people? Not only those made in the customary manner, but all of those *un*made, by hand, later. Experience has demonstrated it is easier to *un*make an adult than make one. The child is still there for the asking, embalmed in the grown-up. To make a comeback he needs only a hearing. This we have arranged. The grown-up is the person who listens to the child.

A lot of people over forty have screwed things up: some of whom are eager and willing to admit it. A lot of people under twenty would like to straighten things out: most of whom are eager and willing to declaim it. This is highly regarded by those over forty as proof positive of total involvement. All the youthful rebels really want is what the aging squares somehow failed to lay hands on — Love and Joy, Brotherhood, Truth, and Lasting Peace.

So what is holding things up? It could be no more than the passage of time. The father says to his son, "When you are my age —" and the son replies, "I'll *never* be your age!" A passage of time separates what only time will join. In the past this confrontation was settled, inevitably, on the side of age. In the new dispensation, survival is possible without actually betraying childhood. Stay as sweet as you are as long as you can: put off growing up.

LADYBIRD

GO HOME TO YOUR

WORM

This sign was carried as a greeting to the President's wife on a visit to San Francisco. It combines, in the modern manner, the candor of the sick joke and indecent exposure. It is "fresh," it is "cute," and there is something about it that is both new and familiar. It is the placard that is fresh. The cruelty of the barb we know to be old. As children, so we taunted the aliens in our midst. The Wops, the shanty Irish, the Polocks, the Bohunks, the Negroes, and the Jews. There is nothing like the barbed shafts of children for bite and cruelty. We fear and envy their uninhibited candor. The child is free — as the adult is not — to speak its mind. It gives no thought to other feelings than its own. Until recently, the innocence and cunning of the child were more appreciated than its perversity. But the child need not just speak as a child. It is the ideal mouthpiece for the child-in-man. The placard that is part of the modern scene is the ideal medium for such a message. Four-letter words and taunts. Verses about ladybirds and worms. This old and familiar scene is made new by the voices of children of all ages. They cannot be silenced by a shocked neighbor, or their dirty little mouths washed clean with soap. They are free, as they have demonstrated, to speak their minds. When the shock of the performance wears off it is easier to judge the caliber of the mind behind it. With our blessings, the child-in-man now speaks for the man.

It is a demonstrated fact that if children are to play and enjoy the carefree pleasures of childhood, others must stop their play and just stand around holding things up. *Holding up* is the natural posture of the grown-up square. If he gives it up he fears the walls will come tumbling down. These fears are not idle. Often enough they have. When he is challenged as to why he takes such a ridiculous posture and seems to live in fear of imaginary evils, he invariably says, "When you are my age —" which is hardly a recommendation. Who wants to be *his* age? Not to be his age becomes a goal in itself. The pursuit of happiness is to stay as you are, to grow down, not up.

Whether the grown-ups trouble or not to look, the heart of the child is on world-wide display. The child's eye view of the world is the international view. To many parents and squares it would come as a shock that another *view* is possible. Who but a child would want to view it? Who but a child is qualified to face it? Properly defined, the educational problem is to keep this view in its proper orbit — out of this world. In Stockholm, Copenhagen, London, Paris, Peking, and the emerging world of the campus city, the child's eye view of the world is the one that cuts through the conflicting views of the surrounding culture. It is basic. It demands only basic things. Love and Joy, Brotherhood, Motherhood, and a Lasting Peace. The unquestioned virtue of these goals silences both informed and misinformed opposition. Dialogue is expendable. What is there to discuss? A few evil men, a few evil forces, need merely be replaced with good men and good

forces. This will remedy such problems as the world is
obliged to face. In this tableau Senator Kennedy, JFK's kid
brother, is the necessary totem figure, and the image of
youth that he provides can hardly be exaggerated. He represents, he embodies, he gives flesh and substance to the
point of view. All that is necessary is to put him in the
driver's seat. Senator Kennedy seems well aware of his
position, and the risks involved in his image, but he can do
little to evade the role for which he has been *chosen.* It is a
matter of time. It is possible, if not likely, that the point of
view will not seriously alter, but it is highly improbable
that this will be true of Mr. Kennedy's image. He cannot
help growing older. He is also committed to growing up.
The conflict between the man and the boyish image is
paralleled in the predicament of his public: they too must
alter. They must grow up or put up. Between the draft and
the nursery, the world and the campus, the lines are increasingly toward communication, with the dropout testi-
fying to where these lines have broken down. The dropout,
by his example, is the first to vote NO! For good or ill, he
has proved himself old enough. It is the first, and may be
the last, effective vote he casts. He votes a solid NO ticket
to what he interprets as the world *out there.*

When the American male defaulted to the
woman, relinquishing his role as head of the family, he
established the pattern of the *default* in family matters of
guidance and authority. How — the grown-ups ask — accept responsibility for their children's lives? Who are they
to wield such authority? Having personally failed to do
the impossible — pursue and cage the American dream
— they are hardly in a position, they feel, to map this
adventure for their children. When accused, they feel the

bitter truth of the accusation. Didn't they *fail?* Of course
they failed. What else can be done with the impossible?
Ironically, it is the best of American parents who feel hu-
miliated by this confrontation. They are informed, literate, and childlike enough to recognize its truth. So who
are they to speak? To question the nature of such great
expectations is paramount to an act of treason. What sort
of dream of life is it that does not aspire to the impossible? Not American, that's certain. On this fundamental
question both accused and accuser are in profound and
steadfast agreement. The American flesh is weak, alas,
but the dream is not. The American parent may fail, but
the dream is impregnable. If it is on these principles the
adolescent rebels, and openly indicts the grown-up as a
failure, the respectable parent, admitting the charges,
takes pride in the child's uncorruptible dream. Dad may
have muffed it, but Son is a chip off the old block. In this
manner, England's angry young men squeezed belated
tributes from the old guard intellectuals they were fiercely
beheading. The Sitwells, among others, were so gratified
to learn that these uncouth young rebels could *both* read
and write, they were eager to praise the erratic solo flights
of many birds still too young to fly. The rebellion comes
both naturally and easily. This gives the nongrown-up
point of view its coherence. One *is* it. One hardly needs to
be it. The problems emerge later. They prove to be old
ones. They also prove to be intractable. This is where the
men are soon distinguished from the boys and the lines of
the battle are drawn. The child withdraws and remains
intact, or becomes a part of the world *out there,* the child-
in-the-man.

The adolescent estate is international in scope, with its
own totems, taboos, and fashions. The youthful Red
Guard rioting in Peking share with the sit-ins in Berkeley,

and the preach-ins in Chicago, a fraternity that lies too
deep for words. They don't like things as they find them.
They propose in this manner to change them. They are
outsiders. They want to come in on their own terms, or
they will not come in. There is no hurry, since the culture
they reject feeds, tolerates, and unites them. A successful
rebellion — absorption by the squares — would have the
effect of dissolving the corps. Unfortunately, the affluence
that underwrites and sustains the movement is also
responsible for its corruptions. External problems and situations have been shifted to internal sensations. The
"trip" has taken over from the "march." The ambivalent
double-talk of the junkie reflects the new estate's double
standards. The freedom to cool it, to burn it, or to forget it,
testifies to the continued noninvolvement with the world
"out there." The hard core of hippies, the movement's fluid
center, is similar to the nomadic culture of gypsies, with
roving ambassadors whose function is to colonize new ter-
ritories. One hippie usually testifies to the nearby presence
of a hive. They have a costume, a language, and they sing
and dance for their supper. No campus city is complete
without a hirsute tribe of these troubadours.

The impulse to rebel is a part of adolescence and perhaps the crucial rite initiating adulthood. The fate of all
these rebellions has always been the same: the rebels
grow up. The novelty and power of the present situation is
that the rebels have sensed where the trouble lies. Strictly
an error of tactics. Many were guilty of growing up.

In the past it has been difficult, if not impossible, to
keep most rebels from growing older: from defecting, that
is, to the enemy. It is currently not only possible, but fun.
There is both a place and a career for nongrowers up. The
new estate is tolerated — like so many rebellions — as
the lesser of many evils: a diversion of forces that might

otherwise prove seriously disrupting. In less flattering terms, the new estate is a playground where the rebels play with themselves. They rock and roll, they teeter and totter, they hoot and holler, they talk and listen, and they occasionally go on madcap safaris into the world out there. These contacts reassure the "serious" players on both sides that they are "with it." That the Peace Corps is promoted as an adequate outlet for the "idealism" of the American youth is a phenomenon that defies comprehension unless seen from the precincts of the playground. The balloons of Hope are released. The Easter eggs are hidden. The children are released to see what they will turn up with. The spectacle is said to lift the hearts, and hopes, of the observing world.

This may seem strange, but it is not mysterious. A few lingering superstitions to the contrary, the adolescent is what the grown-up American secretly longs to be: the fulfillment of his yearning is a dream of not growing up. To remain forever young in mind, in body, and in heart. Fortunately, that is still an unrealized dream, but much has been achieved in getting the young to share it. And *that* is something new. Not so long ago they feverishly hungered to be grown-ups. They were out of their minds to be fathers and mothers, doctors and firemen, heroes and martyrs, scientists, explorers, and even President of the United States. It can be said they are no longer out of their minds. From the gate to the playground, or from the door to the nursery, they have watched the adults go about their business. They no longer buy it. They produce and distribute their own more attractive wares. They have their own Empire, advertisers, merchandisers, and they have their own captive public. They have their own expanding supply and demand. Of the Great Society's exploding population approximately one-third will soon be under twenty, with strong commitments to remain as young and sweet as they are. That is our own private opinion. They are acting in the interest of the public will.

The world-wide spread of this new order indicates that Americans have no corner on childhood. Everywhere, youthful dreams have been frustrated: everywhere, love and joy have been corrupted. And almost everywhere — until this bold new concept — there has been no alternative to growing up. Now there is. You can either stop growing, or try to grow down. The outward form of this fraternity has borrowed from the hippies certain acceptable, regressive patterns, the long careless hair, the soiled careless dress, or the bizarre crazy clothes *once* worn by grown-ups, costumes taken out of trunks found in attics, or purchased at the neighborhood Goodwill outlet, a source of Mod attire. Thus arrayed, the child plays at being adult: in making the scene the adolescent parodies the grown-up. In this carnival scene, as in the Bal Masqué, it is possible to have it both ways: to look like a grown-up of one's choice, while a child at heart.

In this scene the beard is less a symbol of manliness than an example of laziness: it is not a revelation but a concealment, not a presumption but a role. The regressive nature of the performance is climaxed in the confusion of the sexes. Why be stigmatized as a boy or a girl? Why not just *be*? In the choice of roles the young in heart love to play this gives a new and challenging freedom. One can play *any* role. One can *be* anybody. This makes for a bizarre display of feathers in the open-air zoos of the campus cities, but it also conceals the identity of the players. The world *is* a stage. Anyone with a costume can play a role.

Considering the imponderable advantages of childhood, little wonder the child asks, why grow up? Parents seldom contribute an answer. Dreams dissolve into responsibilities, and who wants them? The doctrine of American life is a Bill of Rights. It is rights that are inalienable, not responsibilities. In the terms of this doctrine it is little wonder that children should be judged the most fortunate people. They are the ideal pursuers of life, liberty, and happiness.

The men who phrased this doctrine were not idle dreamers: they merely took for granted that children grew up. That grown-ups were the normal, durable substance of life. They could not conceive that a child's dream of life would increasingly prove to be sufficient, and the loss of such a dream be judged the same as the loss of life. They could not conceive it, but in some quarters it has come to pass. We default to the child's taste because no other taste has proved to be so contagious. The child can now make a song, or a singer, or a book, as it makes the scene. Responding to this intact, expanding market, advertising makes the child the arbiter of fashion. The very, very young, at their realistic war games, mimic both the old and the young at heart. In the Beat Corps, the Brain Corps, the Drug Corps, the Peace Corps, the aging young put the whole thing off. It is a matter of feeling. You're as young as you feel, and they feel young. The poets who speak to and for them need not be concerned with grown-up taste. Bob Dylan's rock-folk doggerel, the double-talk of the junkie, form a new Child's Garden of Verses. Sympathetic intellectuals, posing as elder statesmen, find this ready-made audience made to order. It is sufficient if the leader believes in *them* more than they believe in themselves. It is not necessary that they understand their leader, but that he understands them. Of their numerous spokesmen Mr. Norman Mailer speaks with the clearest voice and with the least calculation, since he speaks for himself. It is his talent, and it is a large one, that he speaks out for two generations of rebels who have not grown up.

> There have been too many fights for me, too much sex, liquor, marijuana, benzedrine and seconal, much too much ridiculous and brain-blasting rage at the minuscule frustrations of a most loathsome literary world, necrophilic to the core —

Nongrown-ups in the tutelage of Mr. Ken Kesey, and the guruship of Dr. Timothy Leary, will find Mr. Mailer's indulgences amusing. They derive from Mr. Mailer's reluctant admiration for the old maestro himself, Hemingway. This "impersonation" stands as an improvised tribute. The aging gladiator (36) naked but not dead, propped on his stool in the TV corner, marijuana ravaged, nicotine stained, shaky with benzedrine, dopey with seconal, and goddam nearly out of his literary mind at the friggin', nonappreciative literary world. The pitch is Hemingway's, but the frustration is Mailer's.

> You can see then that this collection of pieces and parts of advertisements, short stories, articles, short novels, fragments of novels, poems and part of a play comes to be written, after all, and for the most part, on just such a sweet theme — the shits are killing us, even as they kill themselves —

Mr. Mailer's art may well represent what can be done with a writer's frustration, a child's disenchantment, and a man's sense of his impotent rage. It is surely a subject for talent, but talent will not transform it into a great subject. The child so grievously swindled, the artist so foully corrupted, strikes back with a child's instinct for vengeance, a child's fantasy of revenge on all grown-ups, and the grown-up world.

> . . . for one murders not only a weak fifty-year-old man but an institution as well, one violates private property, one en-

ters into a new relation with the police and introduces a dangerous element into one's life. The hoodlum is therefore daring the unknown, and so no matter how brutal the act, it is not altogether cowardly.

The total lack of concern for the victim, the total self-indulgence in the act of daring, is the sweet theme of the vengeful child's audacity. The danger of a man's commitment — on the contrary — is that he knows, and too well, just what he must dare. There is no place in it for impersonation. A man's audacity is rooted in the possible. Speaking of Mailer and Kerouac, Alfred Kazin comments:

> . . . one finds this same loneliness of emotions without objects to feel them about, this same uprush of verbal violence which, when one looks at it a little closely, seems to be unnaturally removed from the object or the occasion. Kerouac, indeed, writes not so much *about* things as about the search for things to write about.

No dialogue has as yet proved possible between those for whom death by daydreaming is a form of salvation, and those who, on realistic terms, prefer life in this world. If we compare this demonism with Céline or Genet it is an absurd, amateur performance. It is staged to upstage the startled squares — to frighten the wits out of the grown-ups. *The shits who are killing us* so often prove to be those princes of the nether regions, our parents. Concealed behind the arras, damn their eyes, are Mom & Pop.

Implicit in our inalienable Bill of Rights is an unsinkable Bill of Wrongs. We cannot cry havoc as to what it is that ails us, since that would be treason. It is our dreams that kill us. They have proved to be too rich for our blood. Our Bill of Wrongs proves to be a frustrated Bill of Rights. What instinct for the facts insisted on the *pursuit* of happiness? So long as happiness remains elusive, one can always flee from nonhappiness. If pursuit proves to be unrewarding, there is flight. For the child-in-man the torments of hell are centered in the zoo of family life, and the prospect of spending *all* of his life in such a cage. Not to grow up is Happiness. Flight from the world of squares is Happiness.

How much of our literature, and how many of our ills — now exported as Democratic doctrine — derive from an overestimation of ourselves that finds its cop-out in the game of flight and pursuit. It gives the illusion of substance to our prevailing disenchantment with life. The youth who pads around the street with a placard has dirty feet but a lily-white conscience: the hood of a tram protects him from the big bad world *out there*. He questions the failure of squares to level with their dreams, but he never questions the dreams. He takes pride in leveling with his peers, but he feels no need to level with his illusions. When the nongrown-up wins our hearts, which is often, it is in the role of the eternal Huck Finn thumbing his nose at Aunt Sally's authority. The great good place is still out beyond the fence loose enough to shuck a boy or a dog through: that's where it was and that's where it still is for the boy and the dog. Some fifty years later a boy from Duluth, Minnesota, whose dreams were colored by his reading more than his camping, put down his own indelible impressions of a vanishing world.

> And as the moon rose higher the inessential houses began to melt away until gradually I became aware of the old island here that flowered once for Dutch sailors' eyes — a fresh, green breast of the new world . . . face to face for the last time in history with something commensurate to his capacity for wonder.

In this transforming light the inessential houses still melt away. It may have mattered to Gatsby, but not to us, that the dream was already behind him, where the dark fields of the republic rolled on under the night. We *know* it is behind us. It is part, as we say, of our inheritance.

More manly, as it naturally becomes him, a man who dips his hands into life, not books, Hemingway stands in the clear running water of his own inviolate Eden. From it he will dip water free from pollution, and reel in trout that defy corruption. His big, two-hearted river is out of this world, safe in his books. The child-in-Hemingway, the man, is the *essential* part of his personality. To spare this child needless corruption became his man's life's work. We can say that he succeeded. The child-in-Hemingway was kept safe from corruption. The actor in Hemingway profited from it, the man in Hemingway suffered from it, living and dying in the shadow of a boy's wounded dream of life.

Before it became an in-law room, then an outlaw room, and finally a soundproofed cell for young swingers, the nursery was the first place to look for the great American classics, the larger number well and widely known as children's books. Nathaniel Hawthorne, Mark Twain, and Herman Melville, hand in hand with the works of Walt Disney. The way things *once* were, and the way we want them to go on being.

The irony of this is perhaps lost on the parents who come down to flush guests out in the morning. Yet we know, in our fashion, that we store our lives in the nursery and the attic. In this wise we seek to secure the future, and preserve the past. Sandwiched between both nursery and attic is the ineffable, mortgaged present, a house children will remember as the days of their captivity.

The American novel, and the American adolescent, seem to emerge equally from the nursery and the attic. The immediate present is a distracting blur as the slides shift in the projector. The American Dream is the technicolor view from the nursery. What does the child see? What he clearly sees is that the grown-ups have sold out. What he fails to see is any worthwhile reason for growing up. Mr. Mailer has graphed this process in his analysis of the hipster and the beat. The stairs of the nursery are bloody where the hipster makes his stand on the landing, knife flashing: they are worn but clean where the beat, Indian fashion, squats plucking his guitar. Both the world *up*stairs, and the world *out* there, is a world of squares and impostors — a world of how things are, totally unrelated to how they should be. This concept of the world is congenial to the child who must put up with the man, and the man who secretly identifies with the child.

This is why, unstated but implicit, we have agreed that children make the best people. They make the best people because they are young and one cannot imagine them growing old. They are not yet washed up, screwed up, or cracked up, and one can hardly imagine how they will grow up. They have great dreams, long, long thoughts, and worried parents. These parents know in their hearts that the children have nothing much to look forward to. The future is just more of the same old blarney or something too ghastly and horrible to mention. It is the child who has had the best of all possible worlds. It is the child who has had the clean fun without the dirty pain. It only stands to reason that sensible, clever children would one day realize this and come to their senses. Many have. They constitute the new fifth estate. What a place it is! No wars, no taxes, no grown-ups, and no old age pensions. It is bounded by the rumpus room on the west and the bar on the darkened corner, where the sign reads

NO MINORS ALLOWED

They are sensitive to signs, and it might be why so few of them have taken to drink.

V: *Going Crazy in Miami*

Dear Abby: A daughter who was very much concerned over her mother's sudden drinking problem wrote, "Abby, why would a loving, respected grandmother turn to alcohol after all these years?"

Had that daughter reread her own letter, she would have discovered the answer. She wrote: "Mother started drinking a few years ago when dad retired."

I know exactly how she feels. My husband is also retired, and I'd drink, too, if I could afford it.   GOING CRAZY IN MIAMI

Why would a loving and respected Grandmother turn to alcohol after all these years? How explain this instant transformation of character? If there's one thing in the world Grandmother had, besides Grandfather, it was character. Now she has Grandfather and the bourbon that sells for $2.98 a fifth.

On the south rim of the Grand Canyon I stood in line for a seat in the grill. A place was finally found for me near the window where a white-haired, gently befuddled old lady, the inspiration of numberless magazine covers, put down a packet of postcards and Indian curios to leave her tip. She had fifteen cents between her gloved fingers, but on seeing *me*, she upped it a dime. Why would a loving and respected American Grandmother do something like that?

This gentle, photogenic lady was the spit and image of my own fictions: it would not have surprised me if she had paused to check my tie, or pick the lint off my sleeve. Skeptical concern for the fumbling male child gleamed in her eye. These eyes, the straight and narrow of her mouth, the brief, telling glances I caught of her handbag, revealed a woman who had come into leisure after many decades of mastering life: a woman who had made it the hard way, and could tell you a thing or two about it. About life, but not about leisure. No, leisure would be her undoing, leaving her to drift and wreck on the reefs of tipping finance. In the vast becalmed sea of leisure she was rudderless. Curios for the young, greeting cards for the old, convalescent cards for the sick or bereaved, kept her — as her children would say — occupied. And there she was, amiably mindless, all of the wisdom of her life impounded and out of her reach since it was no longer in her hands. Now they were gloved and given over to postcards and small change. The school of hard knocks, the life of experience celebrated weekly on *Bonanza,* had left her totally unprepared for the new soft life. Grandmother is the pale-faced fossil on the white man's new Leisure World reservation. She makes afghans: she makes trouble: and sometimes she makes hell.

In the family of American characters I consider the old folks my special province. I take them in, like old umbrellas, and after a few repairs put them back into service. Out of accumulated parts I sometimes make up one from scratch. I often feel I am confronted with my own handiwork. How much should she tip? It seemed to me I knew better than she did. If I put *my* mind to it, *she* would do it. As simple as that. Character has its origins in the fictions that we like to keep around us, a largely imaginary landscape peopled with clichés and bounded by illusions. They make it hard on the eye but easy on the heart. Had this historically respectable process come up with the characters who now crowded the looney bins of Miami? Grandmothers who started drinking Old Grandad a few hours after dear old Dad had retired? Character — what we know as character, what looks, and feels, and smells like character — is an obstruction to the colonization of the brave new world. The Grandmother who says, "Is there something I can do?" is the first to be shot. Those who say nothing, those who take to knitting, nose-picking, ear-pulling, hair-twisting, or rocking, will end up taking to the bottle whether they can afford it or not. There are worse things than going crazy in Miami, and that's going without a drink.

Grandmother is my fiction. I know her. I have gone into retirement with her. But I don't understand her. She should be bigger than going crazy in Miami or she's let me down.

It is possible that Grandfather is doing better, but he is not so addicted to writing to Abby. We don't know. He may well be too drunk to write. But on the smattering of evidence on hand the leisure world appears harder on Grandmother. She doesn't pitch horseshoes: she doesn't sneak off for a round of golf. When the chores are done a game of pinochle might help to kill the time till bedtime, but without the chores to be done who can play cards? Like the shell in the rock, Grandmother is trapped in her character. In so far as she has it, she dassunt change. A corset of character holds her upright in the armless rocker with the wired rungs, her foot audibly tapping the loose board on the porch. It is a classic tableau: flies buzz on the screen, and Grandfather, shirtless, sits on the porch step letting the drip from the leaky hose water the grass between his feet. He hoses the elms, and the leaves rain softly on the brick walk. As dusk falls, the scene shifts to Miami where Grandmother, in the glare of the streetlight, a fifth of Old Crow on the porch beside her, takes from the pocket of her plastic apron a pad and a ball point pen. *Dear Abby* — she writes, "Going crazy in Miami, wish you were here."

Character: rock-ribbed, unchanging, true-blue, blue-blooded American character. We have a place for it in our novels: do we have a place for it in our lives? We do. It is one of our standard brands, our graven images. Appropriately, Old Grandad will help Grandmother survive Miami. For the man and woman shaped by their experience, there is the problem of finding a place to rest it. The leisure world is a shelf. Those shaped by meaningful chores resist idle distractions. Ready-made gloves do not fit their hands, ready-made clothes their bodies, ready-made shoes their feet. What's new is a source of embarrassment. What fits has been shaped to the character. This relocation of the tribe from what is familiar to what is economical, painless, and convenient, parallels with exactness the relocation of another vanishing American, the Indian. The natural man is increasingly unnatural. The natural life is a matter of opinion. Characters, like shells, pebbles, or driftwood shaped by the honing winds and the tide's flow, look interesting but soon prove to be expendable. They are fossils. Some say they give off a sea sound when held to the ear.

Perhaps the increased life-span of Americans is too great a span for *one* character. At one end of this span, or the other, he will pull away from the foundations — and without foundations what is character? To make the crossing of the modern life-span it helps to have lived several lives. Not necessarily to have led them, but lived them. To know the difference between the relative and the relation. Once advised never to switch horses in midstream, this is currently the fashionable form of survival. Switch horses but don't switch brands. It's less a matter of character than taste. Better Grandmother has no character at all than the life-span type that holds up the traffic. What good is it? Worse, what good is she? She would like to advise the younger generation to go in for anything but what she went in for: anything that would prove to be hard to change. Character should be one of its interchangeable parts. One for the growing years, one for the middle years, and one for the long, leisure years of dying. And there is one that escapes her. It is her children that admit to growing old. It is one of her sons, a boy in his forties, who proves to be too old for the job he has applied for. Too old? How well she knows he has never grown up. The chances are she will outlive him but have little knowledge of the son she buries, her memories and affections dating back to childhood years. What happened? In Miami she has plenty of time to think. The want ads advertise for vigorous young people, and the census prophesies that's what they will be getting. Young people. The largest part of the nation! And what can they look forward to? Early obsolescence. Thirty to forty years of going crazy in Miami or Serenity Heights.

The first American of forty, Mr. Walter Pitkin, began his new life by writing a prophetic best-seller: *Life Begins at Forty*. And it had better! For millions of Americans that is where one life ends. Currently, it labors to begin wherever you are, in Chicago or Miami. A gentleman over eighty recently volunteered for the experiment in human sexual responses. At what age do they become *in*-human? Some ladies over eighty make a new beginning — using the word loosely — at Vic Tanney's. Senior citizens yearly graduate from high school and hustle their way toward higher education, both their experience and their beards many years longer than those of their superiors. The University of Kentucky offers a free education to all students who are members of the Medicare program — the *vita nova* that begins at sixty-five. It is the child who now cries to the baby-sitting oldster, "You better get on with your homework, Grandma!" The director of the program has pointed out that one thousand Americans reach sixty-five every day, and there will be close to twenty-four million by 1975. That's a lot of new lives. Better Educare, and the Fountain of Truth, than twenty-four million people going crazy in Miami, most of whom will have to choose between books and drink. It should be pointed out, however, that Grandpa has been hitting the bottle since he was forty. That's when he got the word that he was too old to change, but young enough to hang on. He's preserved in alcohol, having been obsolete most of his life.

Grandma may lack a suitable place in our lives, but she will have her own niche in our Museum of Great Natural Objects. Along with barbed wire, the gangplow, the reaper, the six-shooter, the oil lamp, and the conestoga wagon, Grandmother first opened, then closed, the West. Her work is done. Her mission completed. Miami is where we put her to pasture. Going crazy in Miami is the last shot fired in the real Wild West. It is too early to say in just what outfit she will enter the museum of obsolete items, but her children mostly favor the earlier fashions. The Model T, for instance, rather than the Model A. It is a fact that Grandmothers come in models, and anyone up on the subject can name the year and horsepower. The streets of Miami still offer the collector something of a choice. The old buckboard model is probably over the hill, except for a few tucked away in the Ozarks, but the apron model, with the pins in the bib, the apron strings dangling to be tripped on, is still to be found at the curtained windows where seeds are sprouting in jelly glasses and the rocker has sawed two holes in the Axminster rug. This old bird is well known for her seasonal plumage and the cry, "What will they think of next!" followed by a toss of the wadded apron over the head. The gesture is symbolic, and perhaps this model should be the one chosen for the museum. Grandmother at the screen, the lip of the porch, or out on the windblown deck of the yard, the wash flapping like sails in a gale that spins the windmill, flattens the grass, unhinges the door to the storm cellar, and blows the very soil that a man plows out of the state. It is there she should stand, hooded like a falcon, her grandchildren sheltered in the tent of her apron, the classic picture of the woman who opened, and closed, the West.

That Bryn Mawr girl I used to know — the first to wear dark glasses in the dark — left the seat of my Model-A coupé strewn with the Bull Durham she dropped while rolling her own. Was it money she saved? She had money. Was it something she lacked? She had me. But she was helpless before something contagious in the style. She rolled her own, inhaled her own, and from flared nostrils that defied description exhaled the smoke that is still pungent in my nose. I've often wondered whose Grandma she is, and what, besides alcohol, she might have turned to. There's no doubt in my mind that she probably started drinking even before Dad retired.

Like Austria, the situation in Miami is hopeless, but not

serious. Grandma's "character," the very source of her distress, deprives her of commonplace salvage operations. In exile or in ruin she remains a "comical" grotesque. She is either indestructible, a Rock of Ages, walled in by cataracts and isolated by deafness, or a Brillo-wigged, blue-tinted senior delinquent more vital and alive in her liberated decline than in her long, inhibited rise. The contrary of the indestructible object, the liberated Grandmother, in the space of the wake, has transformed herself beyond recognition. Neither children nor relations can believe their eyes. Rather than a new life, there is a new Image. The very thing she couldn't bear is the one she embraces. She smokes in public, meets her friends in a bar, roots for the team with the most colored players, sits up for the late show, repeats sick jokes, experiments with contact lenses, considers a face lift less dangerous than a pratfall. Was this the woman Grandpa married, the devoted mother of his sons and daughters? No, with Grandpa that woman lies buried. The children are relieved that he didn't live to see it. Her, that is, her gills painted, the lobes of her ears punctured, her bust gathered, her chin lifted, the marbled thighs on which he never set eyes exposed like the meat in a supermarket. There are quicker ways to go crazy in Miami than drink. Grandma knows. After all, as she says, it is *her* funeral. The children have been told not to send flowers. Going crazy in Miami Grandma enjoys her funeral before she is dead.

In the baby-sitter market the teenager might appear in the role of a Beatle, or a sex kitten. If it's Miami it might pay to ask, "What *model* is your Grandmother?" Buckboard, ironing board, never-bored, or the author touching up the proofs of *Life Begins at Eighty*. It's a question of whose. Where Grandpa's ends, Grandma's begins. Besides Grandpa she has survived the dust bowl, the rose bowl, the punch bowl, and the lawn bowl, but on the evidence Miami is turning her to drink. It is if she can afford it. Going crazy in Miami is the price of character.

VI: *Reflections on the Death of the Reader*

Here in the living room, where a fire is burning, the culture channel on the TV features the bi-monthly review of books. The reception is good. We see the book reviewer, a scholarly man, fondling one of the books up for discussion. He smiles at the picture of the author on the jacket. Several other books, their spines toward the camera, are in a pyramid at his side. The one he fondles is the latest novel by Graham Greene. The reviewer likes Greene, but not this book. It is tired, this book. The last book of Mr. Greene's he read was top-flight Greene and not at all tired. Nobody wants to read a tired book. The question arises, does this tired book mark the end of a brilliant and distinguished career, or is it merely evidence of a temporary sag in the author's talent? That is the question of interest: not his latest novel. We have, in this manner, *dispensed* with the novel and are free to turn to more substantial matters. Is the author finished, or merely tired, like the book? If he is finished, should he stop writing? Is the fading glow on the horizon that of a sun that has already set? Nevertheless, author Greene is a man worth watching — and that is precisely what the listener is doing. *Watching.* We watch the reviewer put the book to one side and say that the price of the novel is $5.00. That's a lot of money for something that doesn't come off. The reviewer suggests that it might be wiser to put that money into the kitty, or send it to Care or the SPCA. Why should the reader pay for anything but the best? Just in passing he comments that too many such books lend support to those who cry the death of the novel, but fortunately not all novels are moribund.

This brings us to Mr. Malamud's *The Fixer.* Like *Herzog, The Fixer* rises above the shortcomings of the previous novels. At $5.95 it is worth every cent of it. With this volume in hand the reader can ignore the groping and experiments of the past, and look forward, anxiously, to what the author might dare to do next. The word *dare* is good. It is both suggestive and accurate. The author has made his way to a summit where the reader knows the footing is precarious. What next? From the summit, what is up? Circumstances dictate some sort of holding action, or a descent in the manner of Graham Greene. Is the author finished, trapped, tired, or merely scared? In this drama the next volume is crucial. In the Pike's Peak Derby where nothing really counts but a writer's peak performance, the very acclaim for his triumph prepares the ground for his decline and fall. Where else, but *down*, is there for him to go? Little wonder, in such a competition, that both time and talent prove to be so short-lived. It is the crackthrough that prepares the soil for the crack-up.

Not all writers of interest are caught in this roller

derby, but failure to play the game, to get in the act, comes at a price. Such a writer is not deemed worthy of serious interest and prime time. Above all prime time. His performance escapes the pattern that qualifies him for the literary Nielsen ratings. He is not caught up in the manic behavior of exceeding himself the next time out. He is not in destructive competition with himself. This compulsive behavior, borrowed from the sports arena, the arms race, and the space program, has already taken its toll of both writers and painters. Mr. Norman Mailer's remarkable antics are those of a mountaineer trapped on the summit. After *The Naked and the Dead,* what next? His public exhort him to rise to heaven: his enemies confidently anticipate his pratfall. It is no contest. Pratfalls carry the day. There is a limit to what can be done on the flying trapeze.

In a circus where such acts receive prime time it is difficult to schedule just another good novel. Both the reader and the reviewer find their bloodier appetites have been whetted. Although it takes Mr. Malamud and Mr. Bellow some twenty years to rise above their early groping novels, all the reader needs to rise above them is to have read the last one. An amazing gift: available to young and old readers and reviewers. Mr. Greene's latest book led one young reviewer to throw the entire corpus of his work into *question* — he didn't like the last one: perhaps he had been deceived by ALL of them. Why not? All the reviewer risks is an opinion. The author, the more celebrated the better, is fair game for one and all to shoot down. The public listens with relief to the assurance that one more author they have not read will soon be among those it is already too late to read.

This disposal of the stages of the author's journey — in particular if it has been a long one, marked by many volumes to record it — is agreeable to both reader and reviewer already far behind in their assigned reading. An esthetic of quick disposal is necessary, and it has been found. There is only time — and money — for the best. That the *best* is available to such a late comer — one who has been spared all that went before it — is a cardinal point in the doctrine. The writer must learn to write, but the reader need only learn to read faster and faster. Ingenious apparatus to speed up our reading is now distributed by book clubs, on the safe assumption that club books are piling up behind slow readers. Institutes that provide new "reading skills" now flourish on the culture market. One is trained to read the "average" novel in an hour: no specific time is mentioned for the *un*-average novel. Reading skills include —

Pre-reading: giving a quick, searching scrutiny to the material to see what it is about and estimate its interest.

Phrase-reading: learning to read in phrases, not words. Taking wider "visual bites" as your eye moves across a line of type.

Skipping: selectively jumping over large sections of material after pre-reading has sized it up.

There are other skills, but these are essential. They are of interest since the problem of *reading* seems to exclude all problems of *writing*. How does the writer take wider "visual bites" or selectively jump over what he has written? These new skills mark the end of the old relationship between reading and writing, between reader and writer. From the writer's point of view the bell tolls for the reader, not the writer of books.

Another apparatus that gives great promise toward the

new fine art of reading is the computer. The computer reads and notes what the flesh-and-blood reader is inclined to miss. Some time ago *The New York Times* reported progress made in this department.

COMPUTERS TURN TO
POETRY STUDY
Milton's Influence on Shelley
Appraised through Tapes

The article went on to say that resemblance between *Paradise Lost* and *Prometheus Unbound* had turned up through computer analysis. It also stated that machine computation enormously lessened the burden on the scholar's paper and pencil. His mind went unmentioned. In summarizing, the report came to this conclusion: "The diction of *Paradise Lost* was organically used in *Prometheus Unbound*, and its presence can be detected only by techniques beyond unaided human capacities." *Beyond unaided human capacities.* How many years ago would this remark have been greeted with scholarly laughter? In this remarkable advance more than Paradise turns up lost. What is to be said of a poem deprived of its poetry?

We are accustomed to reflections on the death of the novel, but I have seen little reported on the death of the reader. One need not be a reader, of course, to speculate if the novel is dead or dying. The less one has read the more likely one has an assured opinion. And whether the novel is dead or not, there is the question of the novelist himself. Is he dead or just dying? Today one can meet him and judge that for oneself.

Literature has been a matter of taste for so long, a taste for literature has been taken for granted. It is assumed, that is, that where we have books there will also be readers. That there is something to do with a book *besides* read it has opened new horizons. Reading a book may dislodge or disturb the opinion the reader is anxious to put at rest. Such as — is it the greatest? Does it fulfill the author's twenty years of promise? Or is it best to spend the money on a Care package or the SPCA? There are ladies, known to me personally, who have waited a decade for the best refrigerator, the perfectly safe juice extractor and electric blanket. They will not find it hard to wait for the author's best book.

One of the melancholy facts of human culture is that readers who hate fiction insist on reading novels, and listeners who are tone deaf insist on listening to music, and viewers who are blind to color persist in pursuing, buying, and collecting paintings. It is such lovers of art, more often than not, who become the influential critics, the celebrated patrons, and the diviners of what is hidden and obscure, since what is obvious and immediate in art is precisely what escapes them. The pursuit of what eludes them becomes a career. This spurs them to research, to classification, to commentaries that displace the work of art itself, and in this extraordinary fashion put an end to their preoccupations. Long before machines were so wonderfully human, there were humans remarkably machine-like, and this might prove to be their golden age. Techniques. Techniques that require *no* capacities.

If the modern novel is threatened with a crisis that will not result in better novels, how much of it may lie with the reader who has lost the time, the will, or the skill to read? Who picks up the check without troubling to eat the meal? The book-hungry buyer who does not read supports that superstructure we call the best-seller, a coinage that continues to testify to the clinical accuracy of the American language. Best-sellers we know they are: best read they are not. Can we imagine the smile on the face of Pasternak on hearing that he is a "national best-seller"? Or the glance it would get us from the eyes of D. H. Lawrence? When we think of such writers, and such books, we are confronted with a different concept of the reader. Until a dialogue exists between the writer and this reader, on the terms established by the author, a book is powerless to speak, or persuade, or do more than level a tipping table. This commonplace fact has become so common we have spawned a new species. The nonreading reader. The dividend that goes along with the best-seller. Is it far-fetched to suggest that the new literacy has debased what is potent in the language? That perhaps it is the *illiterate* man who retains the belief that words have the power of life and death? To the man with that knowledge, who cannot read, the book in his hands may communicate more than it does to the scholarly, informed reviewer, who advises the reader to skip it and send the price of the book to Care.

If the reading of novels is hard to verify, the study of novels cannot be questioned. I doubt if there is a college that lacks a course in what we call the modern novel and a bookstore stacked with bins of paperback books. There are courses during the day for those who think they can read, and courses during the evening for those who fear they can't. Was it the novel, or the reader, who gave rise to this suspicion? The plays of Shakespeare, the poems of Donne, the novels of Sterne, Dickens, Tolstoi, Dostoevski, all were printed on the assumption that the person who was interested could read them. *The Divine Comedy* is quite a complicated poem, with an elaborate symbolic and metaphysical apparatus, but Dante assumed that a literate person would be able to follow the intent of the poem. The idea that books are safes with secret combinations, and poems are ingenious double crostics, is not new, but only recently has achieved the status of a doctrine. Mr.

Joyce and Mr. Eliot gave substance to the notion that the reader needs help "beyond his own unaided human capacities." It cannot be denied that he often does. Such refinements of technique and nuance, however, represent crucial breakthroughs, or finalizations, or on occasion a somewhat over-rarefied talent, rather than the bread, the wine, and the thou of our daily fare. I would guess that the "study" of literature merely attests to the infiniteness of its variety combined with the affluence and leisure that have made millions of people curious. The housewife rampant on a field of books might serve as the emblem of the new dispensation, and it is only fair to say that her problems are not confined to the novel she is reading. There is nothing new in the frailty to let others do our thinking for us, and sit, book in hand, while some mellifluous voice tells us what it means. My sources are a bit hazy, but I would say that it all began with the cave paintings. "And what does *that* mean?" says the voice behind the fire, and the artist found himself at a loss for words. I see him there, his jutting brow clouded, blowing softly on a cooling piece of charcoal. Not too long ago something called the Chatauqua catered to this sort of education, and today, on a wider screen, we have Adult Education Programs. As novelists have been saying for some time, a lot of things change, but not people.

One of these changes is what *study* does to what used to be reading. A student of the modern novel recently asked me — off the cuff and man to man — if I didn't think the trapped fly in one of my books was a symbolic cliché. The Midwest setting of this novel simply buzzed with trapped flies, and so did the book. They were flies when they came to my mind and they were still flies when I put them on the page. They belonged to the scene I was painting like the screen at the door, the way it banged when slammed,

and the view through the glass-flawed window. Flies, dead
or alive, were among the first inhabitants. That they
might also prove to be symbols was not my proper business. When the writing is good everything is symbolic, but
symbolic writing is seldom good. Symbol hunting is the
fashionable safari for the vacationing writer and reader
— a way of killing time.

The overtrained, symbol-haunted reader will not accept
the fly for what it is to both the author and the book. An
actual trapped fly. Such a reader wants to talk about flies
as symbols, not the flies that buzz in the mind like magne-
toes, crawl about on greasy and napping faces, swim and
drown in warm lemonade, strew the floor beneath the
window like popcorn, stick as if glued to lumpy light
cords, and always turn up trapped between the rattling
window and the cracked yellow blind. Before it is made
into a plastic symbol later embalmed in cocktail ice cubes,
this fly is first, last, and always an outraged, mindless,
maddening, and unforgettable actual fly. From intimate
experience with such flies many symbols will still emerge.

What loss is there to the reader if the fly does not
emerge as a symbol? The pleasure in this awareness is
part of knowledgeable reading. This experience parallels
the pleasure we take in the moth or butterfly, in a state of
nature, and the same creature pinned to a board, identified as *tiger swallowtail*. The first impression is elusive,
and evades categorization: it belongs to experience, as the
latter belongs to knowledge. Obviously, the curious mind
craves both, but literature is not the field for the data
seeker. A different level of consciousness seems to be engaged in the student who is studying *The Sound and the
Fury,* and the reader, however naïve, who settles down
with nothing but the book. The student's eye is too often
on the stamen and the pistil, indifferent to the flower.

For some time now the influential review has been one that makes the book itself unnecessary. It has been read. It has either been promoted or liquidated. The culturally inclined person must make time for reviews that he cannot find for books. We can speak with more assurance of a *reviewer's* public than we can speak of an author's public. Readers follow reviewers, and review journals: their highest praise of a book or a play is that they have read a good review of it. Review readers soon find that actually reading the book merely confounds the clear impression left by the reviewer.

Audience participation — the culture game readers play — follows the lines established by review journals. Some writers are *in*, others are *out*. The review editor's problem, based on this understanding, is to find the critic who is *bigger* than the novel in question — whose name and opinion, that is, will speak with equal or more authority. The reader faces this problem of the novel in question: it is the function of the critic to resolve it. From this evolves the practice of the critic ON the book, with the critic receiving top billing. Sontag on Marat/Sade, Trilling on Lawrence, Pritchett on Bellow, Mailer on McCarthy, etc. The *reader's* problem is to find that critic who will provide him with the answers. Who will, that is, qualify *him* as a critic. This is not out of laziness. It is not often out of malice. It is simply that *reading* is no longer necessary to the art of communication. What we want is an informed opinion. That the critic supplies. The literate, sophisticated person picks up the book, like lint, through innumerable *contacts* and rub-offs. He goes to the cocktail party. He meets and talks with the author. As a last resort he takes in the movie. Who needs to read *In Cold Blood* to know what it is all about? It is our new servants, the critics, who will do our reading for us, until we find a greater need, have more time, and acquire the necessary reading "skills." The Big Game reader, like the safari hunter, is in pursuit of the best trophy for his library, a conversation piece he has been assured to be the biggest and the best.

The novel is not dead, and the reader is not dead, but some of us are acting mighty peculiar. The production, merchandising, and consumption of books follow familiar national patterns. It is to computers that we turn for the present state and future of the union. How are we doing? Statistics tell us. If they are rising we are doing better. Comfort has been found in the rising numbers that will buy and discuss a good modern novel — not in the parallel statistic that the nation now boasts fifty million more people. A novel with nothing more than excellence to recommend it can look forward to a sale of less than 4,000 copies. In a culture where numbers have been turned over to computers, this *small* number remains a constant. Books are best or worse-sellers: we are buyers of standard brands. Books are one of the products we consume, just as paintings are now one of the stocks we invest in, their *value* subject to the same fluctuating market. Rails down 2 points, Novels up 1 point, Paintings and Grain futures steady. In this bullish market, where does the reader settle down with his book? In what way, and with whom, does he establish the necessary dialogue? Is it possible that neither the world nor the writer has changed so subtly and profoundly as the reader — a man who waits for the ticker to determine his next buy? In the mass distribution of literature, the bins full of books as they were once full of barley, is there not something that is possibly alien to literature itself, with its passion to particularize, to discriminate, to make unique?

Recently Igor Stravinsky, taking a backward glance, made these comments on the culture explosion.

. . . but don't forget that *Petrushka, The Firebird,* and *Le Sacré du Printemps* have already survived a half century of destructive popularity, whereas, for example, Schoenberg's five orchestral pieces, and Webern's six, have been protected by fifty years of neglect.

Protected by neglect. Implicit in this comment is a profound criticism of the role of mass production and consumption in the arts, and a recognition of the loss, in the public, of the faculties usurped by the reviewer, his eyes fastened on a summit he has lost the power to climb.

VII: *Solo*

A few months before Lindbergh landed in Paris I was seventeen, single, and self-supporting, but my own stab for greatness was four or five months overdue. I took the bull by the horns and applied for a job ordinarily reserved for older, more experienced people. Only boys eighteen years or older need apply, the want ad said. I looked about twelve, which saved me money at the movies, but cost me in the fields of self-promotion. I wore my father's herring bone weave topcoat the day I applied. Samuel Insull had his office in the same building and used the same elevator I would be using. It was crowded, that morning, with older men trying to pass as eighteen-year-old boys.

As I stood waiting in the line some thirty yards long — I remember that it made the turn at the end of the hallway — Mr. Miller, a short thick man who put on carpet slippers when he reached the office, moved along the line, face to face, some low, some high, until he got to me.

"Are you a farm boy, son?" he said.

"Yes, sir," I replied. A barefaced lie. I was born in a town with 2,200 people and its own creamery. Mr. Miller gazed a moment at my country boy face, my freckles, my chipped front tooth, my cowlick, my sky-blue plainsman eyes, and the gold-plated collar pin that supported my tie. I looked at him. A big city wheel and a round one, but still a farm boy at heart. "Come with me, son," he said, gave me a wag of his finger, and I followed him down the hall to his office, the door blocked with aspiring and qualified candidates. Mr. Miller's secretary was the one to bring up the problem of age. She was not a farm girl, but she had two boys of her own. The current office boy, an old man of nineteen, agreed to go on licking stamps, opening windows, mailing letters, until proof of my age had been established. I doubted that it would. My father knew me not at all. My mother had died. Proof that I had been born, as I said, in Nebraska, in the county seat of Merrick County, came as a real eye-opener to me but was taken in stride by Charlie Miller, who knew a farm boy when he saw one, just as he had said.

Some months later Mr. Miller held my legs as I leaned from the window and emptied our waste baskets on the hero passing below. I mean to say that the scene above and below, city and country wide, was all of a piece. The hero and the hero makers are farm boys at heart. Smart ones, with a city glint in their eyes. Smart ones, of the sort that will conquer the world. The world's agreement with this estimate is more than an accidental bit of timing, or a sharing of a superficial sentiment. This country boy, this Lone Eagle, appears out of the blue as the script requires, and single-handedly captivates the world. The deed itself

looks nowhere but toward the future, the mechanical con-
quest of space, but the derring-do, the manner of doing,
looks unblinkingly toward the past. This hero's melancholy has its reasons, he is not the first of a breed, but the
last. What one man can do will henceforth be a challenge
of what he can do with or through others. What he can do
with, of, and by himself, will seldom again captivate the
world's imagination. Perceptibly, this imagination is
changing. It must learn to take its nourishment where it
finds it. Loners are out, except as troublemakers. Lee Har-
vey Oswald was a loner. Other loners, some of them farm
boys, have followed in his steps. The recent history of this
word is the changing history of the American imagination. A man should not contain so much within himself.
His dreams should not exceed the situation. The man who
walks alone is soon trailed by the FBI.

Those who are still farm boys at heart are inclined to be
rebels without causes. James Dean would have made a
good farm boy. Charlie Miller would have liked him. He
was a loner. One of those who dreamed big dreams. But in
the years between Lindbergh's and James Dean's dreams,
dreams themselves had become suspect. They were fantasies. They were daydreams. They were material for inves-
tigation. The very idea of trying to fly off somewhere is a
suspect dream. James Dean was less a rebel without a
cause than a dreamer whose cause was hopeless. What
cause was it? The cause of James Dean: the hero without a part. A very different-seeming idol from Charles
Lindbergh until we stop, dead, and consider. One is a hero
with a cause that is hopeful. One is James Dean. Both
idols are made and stamped Made in USA.

In one movie we saw him, a causeless rebel, in the dark
night of the planetarium, with the man-made heavens and
Milky Way arching above him. In this pervasive gloom the

voice of the lecturer spoke of the vast and indifferent cosmos, the horror of space, the nausea of time, the disembodied light from stars long dead, all causes for wonder from which wonder had been removed. In this vault there is terror, incomprehensible aloneness, and a pity for all merely earthly things. Pity for the one and only, the lonely, unique, and mortal James Dean.

Togetherness — the wolf pack, the rat pack, the in-pack, the out-pack, the hot pack, the cool pack, the beat pack, the square pack — is a coat of many comforts against the ice pack of cosmic indifference. Where does one hide from the fallout of numbers, a shelter, a safe place, a hole of one's own?

"I figure it's worth what it costs me," the hole digger told me, "if it makes my wife feel any better."

He seemed to think it might. While he spoke his eyes were on the gaping hole at his feet. One room, about ten feet square, it would sleep three people plus two cats and one dog. Only the cats presented a problem. They were accustomed to spending the night out. How communicate the urgency of the matter to cats?

The point where we stood facing the sea was ideal for a dream house, and this would be one. It would differ from the usual sort of dream house in that it would not rise so much as descend. Twenty-one feet. With fifteen feet of good mother earth piled on the top. To do this it would dispense with such refinements as porches, windows, and a view. I was troubled by the absence of a porch. Where I came from, and had never entirely left, a house was an attachment to a porch. My first safe place, my own type of bomb shelter, was under the flight of steps that led up to the porch, or in the sifted, powdery dust criss-crossed by the pattern of slats. Alone at last. There I would sit with a nut Hershey bar or a fizzing bottle of strawberry pop.

Through the holes formed by the slats I had my own spatial view of the world. Was it outer or inner? From how far down, or how high up? Things of this world valuable to me were all safely there with me: nut Hershey bar, pop, one skate, a pair of stilts, a cigar box containing tinfoil worth up to twenty cents. I mean to say the idea of getting out of this world, and setting up a new one, is not foreign to me. A safe place, with the accent on privacy. Something of the sort you might expect to find on the moon.

My neighbor raised his eyes from the hole in the earth, then tipped his head back to gaze at the sky. The moon was up there. A little pale and lonely looking, but there it was. From the twenty foot hole in the ground that would be my neighbor's view.

"You think we'll put a man on it first?" he said.

A man on it first? I hadn't thought much about it. He gave me a moment to think it over. The first man on earth must have had his doubts, and I had mine. At that moment, however, gazing at the moon, I had a strange but indelible impression. I could see men on it. Swarms of them. All bigger than life. Something about the air makes it easier to see them than we see ourselves.

"Maybe we're already on it," I said. Although it's customary — and I prefer it — to think of the moon as a woman's property.

I forget his name, but I recall the astronaut whose frank approach to his mission pleased me. None of this glory for country and for science nonsense. Not him. He was playing it for keeps. He was doing it because it promised immortality. While other citizens went about their mortal chores, he would be orbiting in space among the immortals. After all, it's in space we look for the Gods. It's why we lift our eyes when we worship. Up there and out there things are everlasting. Stars, cosmic dust, astronauts, and reputations. I like the Yankee frankness of the approach but, as I say, I forget his name. There have been quite a few shot into space since him. There will be more. Is it possible I won't remember the first man on the moon?

My memory has not always been so weak. It's amazing what I still remember about Charles A. Lindbergh. What he did is not much by current standards. He flew an airplane from New York to Paris. Nonstop. Now they do it on the hour. But the important detail is that he did it first, and he did it alone.

Men are also as good as alone in their space suits and the pressurized domes of their helmets, and I don't question they often feel as alone as they look. Cut off, joined to life by the space cord. Their purpose, after all, is to get out of this world, and they do. They do, but we don't seem to feel they do it *alone*. There are millions, perhaps billions of dollars behind them, numberless scientists, laboratories, and experiments, years of preparation, unmentionable failures, to that audible countdown on the pad. I forget how many thousand tons of thrust it takes to blast them off. Up there in orbit they're as alone as all get out — but alone was not how they got there. The big thing they did was agree to the trip. All the king's horses and all the king's men then went ahead and did it — or tried to.

Charles A. Lindbergh — when I last saw him, from twenty floors above Clark Street in Chicago — even managed to be alone among the tens of thousands jamming the street. I could see that, if not much else, through the clouds of newspaper and confetti. Some of it I had emptied out of the window myself. Five baskets. He was as alone in the street below me as a man in space. That I knew. It was essential to what made him memorable. He got into an airplane no larger than the ones you see in amusement parks, put on his helmet, his goggles, his boy-

ish grin, and flew to Paris. There was nothing behind him
but a lot of people who thought he was out of his head.
That's not exactly true — there was more behind him
than you can feed into a computer — which was why, all
in all, he turned up alone in Paris. I can see him now, just
his head in the cockpit, the breeze from the propeller
whipping his hair, his face tanned, his lips chapped just
the way mine got when I rode with the top down. He
needed a propeller, a one-winged airplane, all the gas he
could lift, and what we call luck, but what he really
needed was what he had within himself. Dreams, guts,
heart, and intelligence. All he had behind him proved to
be handy and he would never have got off the ground
without it, but the reason I can't forget him is what he had
within him. I also had it. A longing to do it, or go it, alone.
I was there in the cockpit when he took off, I made the
trip, and I landed in Paris. Solo. First word, first walk, first
flight, first love.

To do it alone, to go it alone, has more going for it than
team effort. Solo is where we come in, and where we go
out. Behind the tableaus of togetherness it is what we are.
If the duet is a triumph, the solo is basic — but currently
less music is written for it. Solo bits and parts are what we
find in the Hollywood planetarium. It is what we describe
as the star system. Solos were once the big features of both
war and peace, but wars are now sorely deficient in big
solo parts. The wars are bigger, and the cast is bigger, but
there is less place for heroes. We give them medals, but
it's mostly to keep them quiet. The big thing is the team
performance, and the maverick hero might screw up the
works. Not that men are less heroic, but the theatre of
war — as we so aptly describe it — is too vast and complicated to feature the solo performance. It's dated. A
great pity, of course, but that's what it is. Tactically it

doesn't pay to make a fuss over one man when the big thing is the harmony of competing forces. In erecting monuments to the Unknown Soldier we admit to the death of the hero. The staggering absence of the hero in world affairs has long been the subject of the modern novel. There he comes disguised as the anti-hero, or the honest heel. The solo performance has not entirely disappeared, but it has been sheared of all heroic trappings. To go it alone, like the resistance, is to go underground. *Plein air* performances are increasingly part of the world of entertainment. The loner has lost caste in the world of affairs where he turns up as the pathological deviate, the anti-social secret agent, but he has regained much of this lost status as the underground, criminal hero. James Bond, Mike Hammer, and Humphrey Bogart are solo performers in this tradition. They prevail against both law and order as forces alien to the solo performance. But the first and last refuge for the solo artist, and the heroic solo performance, is the *plein air* landscape of high noon in the Western. One man against the forces of evil, the muttering, lynch-hungry, faceless crowd. One man, one horse, one girl, and one irreplaceable image.

If we have a model American, the cowboy represents that model. Some Americans change, like Grandmother; others, less talented, will vanish, but the Model Image will not change: it is permanent. The cowboy is immortal, beyond mortal cares and more important beyond mortal fashions: his open range for some time has been in the sky. He keeps in touch with us mortals, however, on prime time. Things may change down here below, but where he rides a good man is easier to find than a villain. Virtue is rewarded: a man has a choice between a woman and a horse. He has nothing in this world but his hoss, his shootin' iron, and his character. Men have had less and survived, but it puts a greater strain on the imagination. With the horse and the guns there is less to explain. That's it. One can take it all in, and millions do, at a glance. But the formula is nothing without the style. Here, as nowhere else in this world, the style is the man. The precious metal of this image will not bend, or fold, but more miraculous, perhaps, it will not tarnish. Marlboro country will not phase it: dude ranches not corrupt it: the flapping shadow of the helicopter not destroy it. Fashionably updated imitations with under the arm holsters, a way with wild women, and finger-tip 400 horsepower, merely remind the aficionado of the real McCoy. And we are all aficionados. Weekly, if not daily, we ride the range of *Bonanza,* and shoot it out at high noon.

We see him on horseback, a sea of cattle around him, but he has paused in the life of a hero to roll, with the skill of a magician, using no more than the hands God gave him, an immortal cigarette. The Bull Durham pouch dangles at his chin, the noose between his chapped lips. He taps a few grains of the weed into the tissue thin paper (in spite of the sidewind that curls his hatbrim), and then, quicker than the eye, with a cunning sleight of hand the cigarette is rolled, the ends twisted, the tip of his tongue applies the timeless seal. The flick of a splayed nail lights the match, we see the flame cupped in his lean brown hands, and as he inhales we inhale with him the sage, the man's smoke, and the limitless horizon. Earth, air, fire, and water in a classic formulation, seasoned with tobacco, saddle leather, and silence. An all-American daydream born of an all-American style.

Style has made him a symbol, and he will not soon pass into nothingness. He is that hero with a thousand faces whose boots, pants, shirt, and hat just happen to fit us, a legend we can all try on for size. Language and gesture, sign and symbol, the expressive ornament and the bone-clean essential, have seldom if ever been combined with such casual, persuasive perfection. The caveman lacked what matters, the shooting irons and the horse. The saddle itself is his coat of arms and the blanket roll his portable empire. Heigh-ho, silver! With a flick of the reins, no more, he is off. In no other figure but the Indian does form follow function so smoothly. This archetype of the self-sufficient man, who takes on single-handed the forces of evil, is currently limited to assignments on the late, late show or in Marlboro country, the museum where we preserve leading candidates for great solo parts.

In the comparatively real world of daily events the solo performance is a feature of the sports world. The bonus-baby is a preview maneuver to call attention to the performer. Money talks. The sports crowd is not diverted by the elaborate efforts to *sell* the team performance: it came to see the solo, and what it came to see it will get. It also came to see a winner, but its greatest hunger is for heroics. It is no *comfort* to the fan to learn that ten other men figured in the triumph. That makes a win, but it does not make a hero. It is not at all essential to the solo performance. He comes to see Koufax, rather than the Dodgers, and Willie Mays rather than the Giants. He asks only that the odds against his man are the best that money can buy. At the moment two astronauts are orbiting the earth in a manner that staggers the imagination, the eyes of the earthbound hero-famished sports fan are tuned in on the neighborhood performance. The man who can throw a ball, catch one, or bat one farther than the rest.

The single man must now pit himself not against man, or machines, but statistics. This is dramatized in the trial of Adolf Eichmann, one man accused of the murder of six million Jews. We admit the enormity of the crime staggers the imagination. But it does more. It escapes the imagination. Six million is a number the imagination cannot grasp. Perhaps Eichmann is the first man to be put on trial for the murder of statistics. Such data stupefies our minds, but seldom wrings our hearts. One man lost at sea, one child in a wood, one horse in a fire, one kitten down a well — the one to one ratio speaks, as we say, our language. When we go on to one flood, one earthquake, one battle, we are speaking the language of numbers. The ultimate illusion is to speak of one world. In the scale of this panorama the theatre of war is seen in perspective, moderate losses are described as good, if the enemy's losses are heavy. If we are losing only one man to their ten, we are doing ten times better than they are doing. In the language of numbers losses prove to be measurable gains. The most widely played game of this sort is percentage. It goes like this: you've got a country of roughly two hundred million people who are subject to a sneak enemy attack. But thanks to a polar warning system you should lose no more than ten to twelve percent. That's all, ten to twelve percent. Eighty-eight percent are saved to clean up what's left. That's more than enough, according to Dr. Teller, widely known as the father of the H-bomb, to clear the roads and the air, rebuild the factories and the schools, restore taxes, Medicare, and all our cherished institutions to just what they used to be — including war. That's percentage. It gives the heart a lift to play the game. Deaths on the highway, flood, plague, and starvation, hardly add up to more than a statistical tremor — percentage wise. You wouldn't notice it at all if you viewed it from the moon.

A little thought will do for percentages, but it is no help with numbers. The more thought you give to numbers, large ones, the less you grasp. But ten, twenty, forty, sixty, ninety *percent* is not a disaster, just a simple percentage. Something both the criminal and the prosecution can grasp. The percentage is something calculable. The crime is something unimaginable. So we come to what seems to be the heart of the matter: we are no longer confronted with a conceivable horror, an imaginable disaster, a punishable crime. Such things are behind us. We are now faced with what is merely calculable.

If we are dealing with facts we cannot comprehend, little wonder we deal with them so badly, or speak one moment as if we were sane, the next mad. Between factual statistics and paranoia it is difficult to distinguish. With numbers what can we do but calculate? We see the lineaments of it in the decimal system, a way of organizing knowledge and cataloguing books. We have no other means to deal with the phenomenon of outer space. What is it? A calculation. The moon is so and so far, a star is so and so big, the Milky Way is — well the Milky Way, practically speaking, is inconceivable. Under the dark hood of the planetarium the mind feels both terror and wonder. From the loudspeaker drone the inevitable statistics. The word from outer space — if we want it — we already have. It is *data*. One cannot imagine it. We can only calculate.

It is forty years now since Charlie Miller held my legs at the open window, while I emptied the baskets over the hero who passed below. What did we have in common? We were both city boys who were still farm boys at heart. On those scales where dreams are weighed and computed there is not much to choose between our follies — the farm-tik and the luna-tik are both out of this world. One drags his feet in the past, the other blasts into the future. The present is a trap door, or a launching pad, through which both make their escape. Weightless in space we might prove to be timeless. Perhaps it is the pull of gravity that ages and binds us. I still like the Yankee frankness of that astronaut who was taking the long view, and playing it for keeps. I like it, but as I said, I forget his name. It's both amazing and foolish what I remember about Charles A. Lindbergh, the Lone Eagle, who flew an airplane non-stop from New York to Paris. Solo performance. My feeling is he's still up there, and that nothing will bring him down.

VIII: *Face Value*

With a note in his voice that was new to me my father said, "You're not spoofing, are you?" Not to me, but to the pretty young woman with the dice cup behind the cigar counter. No, she was not spoofing. A few months later she became his second wife. The problem about spoofing was not settled, however, since my father frequently asked the same question. Was she spoofing? He could never be sure. To be vague on this point is no joking matter, and not the basis, as we say, of a lasting union. If you don't know when a person is spoofing, what *do* you know? My father had what I considered a great sense of humor, but the spoof never struck him as the least bit funny. He would take off his glasses and rub the bridge of his nose, or pull the lobe of one ear. This lobe, like his nose, had a purple stain from the color his pencils left on his fingers. They were known as indelible, and came with bright red caps, like porters. There was also a stain where my father moistened the point between his lips. This is aside from spoofing, but I mean to point out that I was sensitive to my father's dilemma. Along with me, it was one of many he never solved.

I next learned about spoofing at college, along with something described as a hoax. A hoax is more ambitious than a spoof. A hoax I was in on called for the removal of the screws from the legs of folding chairs, then replacing these screws with kitchen matches. These folding chairs, when sat upon, folded in an extremely unorthodox manner. The chairs, about thirty in number, were involved in the college graduation ceremonies, and occupied the first row, front and center, of the open-air theatre. They were reserved for the president, the speaker, and other notables. We all considered the results a first-rate hoax.

A few years later, in the world of men, I realized I had been gullible and inexperienced. Friends of friends made a career of the *hoax*, and took it seriously. If you were southbound on Fifth Avenue, some thirty years ago, you may have been delayed or redirected one block east to Madison Avenue, owing to the barricades and smoking lanterns that indicated street repairs were under way. A hole about eight feet deep had been excavated, and when finished the workmen walked away and left it. I have it straight from one who held the lantern. Policemen redirected traffic, and there was a good deal to redirect. In the fullness of time this hole in the street proved to be a hoax.

During that same golden summer a small beach house on the Cape, in the dunes west of Wellfleet, was known to have disappeared. A hurricane? There had been no storm. A few wide tire tracks were found in the sand. A generous reward for the return of the house, even in a different color, went unanswered. I once heard of a similar house on the beach near Rehoboth, but who can be sure? In a more subdued vein these madcap boys redecorated a friend's apartment. He was usually stoned, but reputed to hold his liquor well. Over one long summer weekend, working like beavers, they managed to screw the chairs and the bed to the ceiling, then paint the ceiling on the floor with the light fixture burning. When he returned, that's how the owner found it, the dawn light glowing in the upside-down windows.

The perpetrator of a hoax, a joke intended to deceive, has always run the risk of too great a deception. The joker who gets shot, the victim who goes mad, or the innocent bystander who breaks his neck. The successful hoax depends on negotiable face value, in the good coin of the realm. It is not good hoaxmanship, for instance, to "fool" mentally disturbed people. First of all, it's no joke. Their notions of *face value* are in flux. The hoax may be too much like the way things really are. The bumper strips that read

GOD IS ALIVE AND IN THE WHITE HOUSE

vividly illustrate this dilemma. Without a guide on hand who says, "That's a joke, son," how would a stranger assess its face value? In the open market face value is increasingly value-less. If Adlai Stevenson, for example, and not Mr. Alan Abel, had been the founder of SINA, more familiarly known as the Society of Indecency to Naked Animals, the confusion among the intellectuals would be as great, or greater, than that currently among the squares. Face value is packaging, merchandising. The *real* value is what lies behind it. The name, the label, the reputation. If properly born and raised, we know there has to be *something* behind *everything*.

Not too long ago the sophisticated shopper tipped the object in question to glance at the bottom — less for the price than the stamp that would assure him it was imported, and where it was *from*. A dear friend of mine, addicted to object tipping, strolled about tipping objects in a plush apartment while waiting to be interviewed for a teaching position. She was a modern-type abstract painter, and after tipping this object that was how she looked. The block of glass *was* imported, but it happened to be full of ink.

But not all objects can be hefted and tipped: we must accept the package or try to see through it. If President Johnson, while ear-pulling a beagle, had dropped a friendly word for Mr. Abel's SINA, the joke would now be on all of those who once considered the movement a hoax. Animals identified as naked would no longer be exposed. In the absence of assured face value we are obliged to rely on what lies behind it: General Foods, General Motors, RCA, NBC, and LBJ. The hoax is no longer a question of *what* is perpetrated, but *who* perpetrates.

In a statement summarizing the administration's achievements, LBJ recently made this statement:

> When I look back on what we've done for the past three years, I'd say we have more democracy, more prosperity, than ever before. Another thing, there is a better feeling with Canada and Mexico than ever before and if we can live that well with the people on both sides of us, it is a pretty good record for the rest of the world.

Is that a joke, son? The face value of the statement defies commentary. It has to mean *anything* but what it is saying. Is that also true of the man who made it? Nowhere is the problem of face value so acute as in the words, deeds, and face of Lyndon Baines Johnson, who is President of the United States because the voters chose to believe in his *face* value. The *face* value of his experience, his words, and his promises. A nation in an expanding war abroad, with insoluble, demanding crises at home, soberly and optimistically advised that we have good relations with Canada and Mexico. The crisis of the nation is not in Vietnam, or in Watts or in Selma, or the fire next time, but in the profound and disquieting realization of the people that their face-value judgment of Lyndon Johnson was wrong. His face value is *out*. We have no idea what value is in. There are many who feel that they have been the victims of a gigantic hoax.

We now know that certain things shouldn't be mentioned in public because somebody might take them at face value. Like McNamara for President. The suggestion has been made. What we call trying it on for size. The Secretary gave a speech at his daughter's graduation, and a man who has a daughter, and can speak, is of potential presidential timber. The modern teller of tall tales, the perpetrator of hoaxes, must remember that the joke around the water cooler might prove to be no laughing matter. Would you believe Maxwell Smart for President? The agents from Chaos might see it as the smart way out.

In the current liquidation of face value we have the emerging boom of *camp*. The appearance of camp is the death of the hoax as a *hoax*. As camp, however, it may have a new, extravagant life. Camp ends the practical joke, begins the impractical joke without limit. The Fair Trade price we put on face value is a form of camp.

A word of shady origins and associations, at once smart, avant-garde, and faintly disreputable, to the American palate *camp* has the taste Stendhal reputedly found in sherbet: it lacks only sin to make it perfect, and perhaps it is sin. The virus is contagious, passed from lip to lip like the common cold. The interval once necessary to produce

106

an epidemic has been shortened by modern communications. Rashes of camp, at varying levels of affliction, break out simultaneously in Beverly Hills, Berkeley, Shaker Heights, Ohio, and Madison Avenue. Hearing the word *camp* mentioned some will wonder, some smirk, others knowingly smile. In this remarkably fluid condition the word may well be at its top face value. It is currently the game any number can play. The multiple image of the way things are, the suspicions we share as to how they are not, for a moment are localized in this suggestive, imported label. The term is sin-ridden as cheap perfume, or bizarre as Mrs. Gaye Spiegelman, topless mother of eight. It should be taken with music and a knowing guide, as one takes LSD.

The Brillat-Savarin of camp gout, Susan Sontag, lists a random sampling of camp objects. Under the transforming lamps of camp they become objets d'art. Tiffany lamps, Beardsley drawings, Bellini's operas, *Swan Lake,* and turn of the century postcards. To this list we might add, as the camp encampment, the territory loosely known as the City of Angels, the national museum and open-air theatre of camp life. To the often asked and long unanswered question, *What is it?* — we now have an answer. It is camp. In the world of more and better images, camp is the inexhaustible image-maker. As the artist once turned to "nature" for inspiration, the camp artisan need only *think* of Southern California. It is camp *au naturel.* Camp in the pure, like heroin, before it is cut for addict consumption. The scale, consistency, and success of Disneyland is camp for everybody. One cannot only see it. One can be in it. Los Angeles is a continuous camp *happening.* From the encompassing hills (the smog permitting) one can observe a single spectacular production, open day and night like the supermarkets. The cast of millions is enlarged daily. The blood never tires. The young man with his date in the darkened car, who sits groping both for love and the memorable metaphor, will not find it in the sky, veiled off by the smog, or the wheeling arcs of Hollywood klieg lights, but in the miles and miles of wire, blinking lights, spinning wheels, and the communications of the computer. In disbelief we call it the unreal city: the highest praise.

Precisely to the extent the scene is unreal, it is equal to our condition. If panned from the rise, the knowing camp viewer has an infinite variety of objects to choose from, all ready-made. Jolson's mausoleum, Forest Lawn for the mortals, the sidewalk with the handprints for the immortals, ready-made civil wrongs, ready-made civil rites, the nation's first All-Ad radio station. No conflict exists between the media, the message, and the receiver. "We're not ashamed of being scavengers," said the executive of the Golden Gate Disposal Company, "but we do want a better image." It will be supplied.

There is a grievance called Watts, but riots did not put it on the map. It is in Watts that Simon Rodia constructed his happening of shards and salvage. An act. An act of independence. But an imaginative act is not so easily confronted as a riot. The towers of his city can sometimes be glimpsed at the fringe of the TV-panned riot area. That is as it should be: glimpsed in passing, as one glimpses Gaudí in Barcelona.

The problem of Watts — the civil problem — is the communication problem of the conflicting image: the disinherited at home in middle-class houses, with lawns, sprinklers, dying palms, and used cars parked at the curbing. The victim with a grievance finds his circumstances at odds with his "image." A slum rioter without slums: a ghetto sufferer without a ghetto. The Watts slums, appropriate to camp, face the TV cameras with lower-middle-class assurance. In the absence of the riot the viewer wonders if what he sees on the screen is the program's commercial. He waits for the housewife to appear at the door with the bundle of laundry, and speak up for the soap. He waits for Ajax, who is stronger than dirt, to gallop up and off. In this sun-drenched, open-air slum only the riot itself will communicate the message. The ghetto has to be accepted as a state of mind. The Negro, the Mexican, the Puerto Rican, who hopes to make a case for his condition, must first reconstruct the scene in the image of what ails him: he carries the virus but he sometimes lacks (on the air waves) proof positive of the disease. To this extent *on the scene reporting* — unless a civil rite or riot is in progress — does the injured more injury than service. The public image of the sharecropper, harnessed to his plow, the furtive, switch-blade black boy, harnessed to the ghetto, is at hopeless, ridiculous odds with the sun-faded torpor of Watts. Even the riot-ruin seems unreal. Something caused by an earthquake or a plane crash. Surely not the handiwork of people *living* in Watts. Nor can the camera, panning the scene, always avoid the visionary towers of Simon Rodia, an unexampled triumph of what work and talent can make of trash. And something more. An unparalleled example of self-help.

Simon Rodia's monument seems designed to humiliate any group with a grievance, any cause that is impertinent enough to ask for more than it gives. Invisible but palpable in the Watts problem is the environment's failure to support the grievance, the alienation the inhabitants suffer from the face value of their condition. The face lift they have is not what they want. It merely adds to the torment of their ghetto state of mind.

It is no mistake that Cecil B. De Mille, Aimee Semple McPherson, and Simon Rodia all had their visions in the City of Angels. The metaphysics that polarize American life are plain horse-sense and pure non-sense. Pipe dreams, daydreams, fantasies; and visions are price-less precisely because they are face-less. The dealer on the car lot says, "Make me an offer!" He knows the game. He has the picture. He knows, and *we* know, he is a dream merchant, a lying, conniving debaser of dreams and val-ues. With a face value on dreams. If this dream merchant is the last refinement in the deliberate defacement of value, he is an artist in the sense that it is his own face that he begins with. He stands behind — as he says — the dream he sells. On the used car lot the subtle tie that binds the practical joke and face value together finds its ethic, and its dialogue, on the message written on the windshield. After more than forty years I can still see one clearly. It reads:

AIRPLANE ENGINE — SWEET RUNNER

As if I needed to be told. As if I couldn't judge that for myself. A seven-passenger Marmon touring car with wire wheels and class. Simon Rodia, that spring, was collecting raw materials for what would soon slowly emerge in Watts, and Aimee Semple McPherson was collecting souls. My father and I, on Main Street and in the Bilt-more's expansive lobby, were collecting dreamers for a trip to Chicago. We were all selling dreams beyond price. A young man named George Young had just swum to Cat-alina and collected Mr. Wrigley's $25,000, and swans were floating on the popcorn-strewn water of Echo Park.

A gentleman pressed between signboards, like a sand-wich, advertised what I no longer remember, but knew to be a great and appealing value, on the *face* of it.

That much has not changed. There is today more face value than ever before. The face *lift* makes possible the negotiable redemption of lost time. The façade is hardly an American invention but what else presumes to do so much for so many, and makes of face value a way of life?

IX: *Understanding McLuhan*

By the same token, and I am just beginning
to think about this while I stand here . . .

MARSHALL MCLUHAN

In a world preoccupied with the problems of war,
the morning news brings word of peace: peace in outer
space. This unparalleled agreement prohibits all states
from placing nuclear arms, or other weapons of destruction, in an environment empty of, and deadly to, human
beings. So there is hope. If you can get into outer space
you're safe.

Word also comes that Sveti Stefan, a walled Dalma-
tian fishing village so beautiful it lies beyond the telling of
it, has been transformed into a lively resort and its sleepy
inhabitants "relocated" elsewhere. That is the word, *relocated*. We are experts, we moderns, at relocating people
and establishing resorts.

To understand McLuhan it is merely necessary to understand the world. The problems of comprehension are
much the same. The commonplace proves to be extraordi-

nary and the mad prove to be wise. Both peace in outer space, and those who will enjoy it, are very much at the heart of his considerations. What makes men tick? What are the wild space waves saying? In outer space, as of this morning, it's peace. In inner space, currently, it's McLuhan. Understanding McLuhan may prove to be the greater risk.

In his expressed affinity for *Finnegan's Wake*, a wonderland of pun, play, and paradox, we have such key as we need to the McLuhan method. This is made explicit in *The Medium Is the Massage,* where he whimsically puns on himself. Does he mean to be taken seriously? That too is up to the reader: or perhaps one should say the player. The truth might turn up on a role of the dice. McLuhan relies heavily, as does Joyce, on the participating reader as a work force, an essential element in the hoped-for creative act. For many participants it will be the first, and possibly the last, swing on the flying trapeze of free association. Some find it, and rightly, exhilarating: some find it, and rightly, a bit nauseating. The square who swings with McLuhan is at once both hot and cool.

His special gift, and it is no small one, is for the orphic utterance, cryptically brief. We sense a truth that is implied, rather than stated. He is not too concerned with what he thinks, or means, since it is what *we* think he means that matters. This is often true in the art of prophecy. Without exception, he is provocative to the extent that he is cryptic. When he explains what he means, all is lost.

As the style is the man, the McLuhan style is better heard than seen. On the page it blurs. On the panel discussion it glows with a neon flame. It has its origin in, and directs itself to, the audiovisual field of *communications.*

There is a public that sees the McLuhan face as it hears the McLuhan message. "I'll talk," he says, "and you tell me what I mean."

This is a fresh and provocative approach to the field of extrasensory perception. It is McLuhan's field. We can neither pin him down nor tune him out. The style is at its best in excerpts, panel discussions, TV interviews. In this context the fragment often sums up and surpasses the whole. It is provocative to hear that school actually obstructs a child's education: that it interrupts the intense process of learning that goes on in the outside world. This seems to be true until we give it some thought. Unhappily, no child is more obstructed than the one we describe as a "dropout." School does not interrupt his education — nor does the world outside begin it. Education is more than the McLuhan observation would lead us to think. Education is still applied effort as well as unconscious absorption. The McLuhan game of thought is a shell game that frequently conceals the pea of substance: our eye is intended to be on the legerdemain, and that is where it is.

The medium is the message, among other revelations, shows the deft hand of "creative" advertising. General Electric would pay well for, and hardly do better than, "the light bulb is pure information." The McLuhan aphorism and the singing commercial have more in common than prime time, and both may prove to run the same risks of early obsolescence. The phrase most readily appropriated is also the most easily liquidated. We will have had it. We may, indeed, have already had more than we think. Why else would Mr. McLuhan pun on himself? Having tried it on for size, he is slipping it off. His tone is that of the after-dinner speaker sufficiently experienced to dispense with his notes and turn in a good performance with whatever comes to mind. A good deal does. The medium is the art of it. Bells appear to ring and horizons widen until the Master explains just what it is he means. That caps the performance, and at the same time dispels the illusion. It *is* a performance. We *do* seem to grasp more while the balls are in the air. McLuhanisms have their rise, their life, and their fall, in this period of willing audience collaboration. He is the medium. For the message we must tune in on ourselves.

There is method in this madness, and there is also a skillful cop-out. If the meaning falls through we have only ourselves to blame. A central point in the McLuhan doctrine, and fundamental to his performance, is that we are chronically blind to the Emperor's new clothes, and see him forever in his old ones. But in the act of demonstrating what it is he sees, it is old clothes that he exhibits, centuries of old clothes. Art and literary history inexhaustibly provide him — as they do any researcher — with parallels that confirm his own position. This show of learning is stitched and stapled together with the familiar academic apparatus: "As Cézanne was first to show . . ." "Historians agree . . ." "The student of the history of the clock will find . . ." It proves to be an erudite, but not a scholarly, demonstration. He runs a rake through the bins of history and hastily assembles his own collage. This pads out and weights his thesis, but discredits his performance. Pure information may describe the light bulb, but it does not comprehend McLuhan. History supports any man with the point of view that media provide numberless extensions of man, but it does not support the McLuhan understanding of media.

> Persons grouped around a fire or candle for warmth or light are less able to pursue independent thoughts, or even tasks, than people supplied with electric light.

Is that the pure information we get from the light bulb? If we try it on for size, who does it fit? Over thousands of years most of our independent thinkers have pursued their thoughts by sun, fire, and starlight, blithely unaware of their great media handicaps. Thought, for these primitives, was naïvely believed to be a form of light in itself. Where intense, the most illuminating light of all. *Let there be light* is an invocation to thought before it served as an appeal to the local power company. Just as McLuhan can exalt audience participation without reference to the mystique of Adolf Hitler, he can flatly state that persons in dim light are less able to pursue independent thought than those in the glow of a mazda. The contrary opinion has more to recommend it, and all of recorded history behind it. In this example McLuhan seems blind to what is "light-productive" in his own practice, the laser-beam in the surround of darkness, the sparks provided by reluctant material. Persons grouped around a fire or candle for warmth or light may be more *inclined* to think than merely gather information. Persons oversupplied with light have a yearning for the dark. In the dark — and where better? — one can nourish the flickering flame of thought.

By his own example, McLuhan is best the less pure-light-bulb-information he has around him. When he relies on the faculties of the artist — intuition, imagination, and free association — he is frequently both audacious and perceptive. When he then continues, as a deep thinker and scholar, to encrust his position with armor, the life-enhancing and light-producing elements are extinguished. The historical script is poorly adapted to his updated eye and ear-catching performance.

> By the same token, and I am just beginning to think about this while I stand here, crime has become obsessional in our society as a form of artistic expression.

This message is sharp, but it is the medium that wins our hearts. *Beginning to think about this while I stand here.* Isn't that how, in our hearts, we would like to solve the big ones, and feel that we must? While we stand here. In a flash. And the light to this flash is McLuhan. It is no small service, and may well prove to be enough. It is at these moments of improvisation — casual, whimsical, and occasionally inspired — that his media and mercurial message are the most effective. When he pauses to explain what he means, all is lost.

In an article that summarizes this thought, published in the *American Scholar,* we have the essence, free of the excrescence, of McLuhanism. It is a provocative and indispensable statement. Fresh thought on many issues must start from it. From many of Mr. McLuhan's public statements I gather that he would judge such results as sufficient. The problems arise in his willingness to endlessly improvise on what *he* thinks he *means,* as well as on what *we* think he *means.* This makes for discussion, for McLuhanism, and a choosing up of sides where no lines actually exist. This may well popularize, but eventually discredit, what is useful in the McLuhan canon. We may throw out a healthy baby with the bath. I judge it unfortunate, however inevitable, that he has been obliged to assume a position, and accept responsibility for many remarkable statements: "I have touched upon the future of language, the future of consciousness, the future of the city, the future, perhaps, finally, of work."

No better definition (noting the descending climax) of McLuhanism will be found. The problems arise in that having *touched* on them, he then goes on to elucidate his findings. In those instances with which I am familiar the diamond is transformed into a zircon. The gemlike flame of *The medium is the message* gives off a diesel smoke.

This does not discredit the provocative insight, but it should deter both enthusiasts and detractors from thinking of the McLuhan performance as a system. Understanding McLuhan has little to do with understanding media.

The media that require McLuhan's understanding are the *extensions of man*. Radio is an extension of the ear, television of the eye, the wheel the foot, the electric circuit the nervous system. The way in which these media have transformed our lives, and our concept of the world, is Mr. McLuhan's subject. His approach is that of the laserbeam, cutting through accretions of pure information, or the sweeping McLuhanism. One such celebrated sweep is *The electric light bulb is pure information.* If this is not staggering in its insight, it is a fresh and suggestive concept. There was something in man-made light we were missing, and this was it. Pure information. Information often does dispel darkness, and so do light bulbs. Carried away by this coup McLuhan goes on to say, "the atom bomb is information, pure electric circuitry." That breaks the master's spell. We sense that the needle is stuck in the groove. "Pure information" and "pure electric circuitry" prove to be impure verbal gimmicks. If we are led to reexamine our first happy impressions the result is disenchanting. The McLuhan structure — and he has one in mind — rises skyward on such shaky foundations. It floats. But that is not so unusual in this day and age. We might describe it as a "happening" in which the public faith supports the emerging towers of theory. Where the light of pure information is dim, the participating audience is called upon to supply it. "More light!" is a call to the bench for fresh recruits. They are not lacking. Daily they seek to explain what the master means.

Unhappily, the orphic aspect of McLuhan thought lends itself to the hypnosis of the singing commercial.

Pure media. Whether it comes from Coca-Cola or McLuhan. *The medium is the message* is as pure as *Things go better with Coke*.

The appeal of the performance lies in the way it cuts through centuries of data, of information, waiting for reclassification. It also lies beyond what is known as demonstration. The great purview thinkers, Toynbee, Spengler, etc., reap their harvests in the past but stake their claims in the future. For the modern media man, glutted with light and information, McLuhan provides an oral purgative. The confusing and disorderly past is reduced to a few orderly essentials. Alice's Wonderland, Disneyland, and McLuhanland prove to have much in common. With a little luck, and a lot more light, we could be happy as kings!

It is characteristic of a good McLuhanism that it often strikes the reader, or listener, as whimsy. Does he really *mean* it? It is a question the author shares with the reader. He isn't sure. He is trying it on for size. In so many words he is saying, "This comes to mind, but I don't believe it." I find that good: even invaluable. It is the free-play, intuitive side of his talent, and profoundly nonsystematic. True believers we always have in abundance: McLuhan is a prophet of self-doubt. At his best he is a salesman who advises the eager and willing buyer to hold off.

His taste for literature, and his respect for literary values, may explain what is contagious in the most celebrated McLuhanism. The medium is the message is an updated version of *The style is the man*. Media has always been and will probably remain the message content of what we call art. In the same way, it works its spells and charms insidiously. The visible and invisible waves of influence that radiate in all directions from the singing commercial have a long and respectable ancestry. Anything with *style* was once a poem, a pillar, a song, or a culture: anything with style is now an Ad. The Hathaway shirt man, with his black eyepatch, Commander White-head with his beard and his schweppervescence, the sub-urban gentleman with his dog, his fireplace, his bonded Bourbon, any young executive who calls from the sling chair, "While you're up, get me a Grant." It is both media and nostalgia. It is pre-McLuhan and before communica-tions. If the Ad has *style,* we have become the Ad. Com-munication differs from propaganda in that the latter takes doing, the former is instant. It may soon be idle to argue which came first, the Ad or the consumer. What song is NOT a singing commercial? If it is sung, somebody will buy it. The quiet homebody type is Indoor Advertis-ing: the loud extrovert type is Outdoor Advertising. In Ad-vertising Ourselves, as Mr. Mailer divined, we are doing no more than what comes naturally. We *communicate.*

The want ad section of the paper tells us
CHALLENGE
is a nine-letter word meaning
"an opportunity to create
through imaginative skills."
Is that media or message?

> Jack Armstrong can't hold a
> job at Fairchild. He's had five
> in as many years. He's been a
> circuit designer, Senior Pro-
> duction engineer, Integrated
> Circuit Application Designer,
> etc. We have a lot of job-hop-
> pers at Fairchild.

That's media. If you're not on the proper wave length all you get is the *message.* It may not be up to Dreiser, or as subtle as Fitzgerald, but the *style* is unmistakable. Only the *right* man will get its message. We hope. This can't truly be said of the Tareyton smoker who would *always* rather fight than switch. Message overpowers medium. A subtler taste for media is cultivated by the chronic watchers of the late, late movies, where an alert and knowing eye is necessary to distinguish between the Ad and the drama. Is it Gary Cooper's or Marlboro's country? Is it the Pepsi or the Lost generation? Media is the presence of more than meets the eye. One way to test our own talent for it is to switch off the sound on the TV commercial. *Where* are we? Can we locate ourselves without the road signs? "Recognitions" is an old American game. Small fry trapped in cars continue to play it with signboards. On the superhighway it is the landscape that reels by, as it does in the movies. We may not understand the fourth dimension, but we live in it. Media is the presence of this dimension in communications. It explains both the poetry and the truth in the way we put the ultimate question: we no longer hope to know where we *stand*, but how things *are*. That is less a matter of geography than *style*.

When Midwest farm boys with a taste for art began to paint mashed guitars and off-center wine bottles — neither well-known Midwest products — they were under the spell of media, not "art." Whatever it was, mandolins, harlequins, dead fish, tipped tables, live fruit, cubistic faces, they sensed that it *worked*. Things that work in this manner also work while we sleep. *Good* communications is a time capsule, a delayed action pill.

It is precisely Mr. McLuhan's talent that he is always saying more than he knows. He knows the media, but the message he leaves to us. On the occasions he labors to clarify, the media escapes in the demonstration. McLuhanisms defy clarification, but they bear the hallmark of instant recognition. We feel their relevance better than we think it. We like the laser-beam audacity of it. If understanding ourselves is to be recommended, understanding McLuhan is still worth the trouble. We are a talented people, and it is our talent he puts on the line.

Up there on the high wire, where the tent darkens, and the figure of the performer is disturbingly foreshortened, Marshall McLuhan holds our attention and haunts our dreams. For how long? We are known to tire quickly. He must keep all the balls in motion. "Look Ma, no hands!" he cries, and we look. We leap as he leaps, we soar as he soars, but it is our own faith that supports him. It is the media, not the message, that keeps him aloft.

x: *The Mind at Play*

I adore simple pleasures. They are the last
refuge of the complex.   OSCAR WILDE

People are spontaneous. They are very
quick and very good at doing little things
that are truer than life.   TONY RICHARDSON

Pot is Theatre!   ANON.

Who would question that the leader of the free
world is a serious man? There is little room, in his work,
for the mind at play. It is his job to rally all our resources
and by waging war preserve peace in the world. As a serious man, it is a good example of his mind at work.

If you are over forty, and if not hale at least hearty, you
are well accustomed to the world of Newspeak. You
learned to speak it as a child. It is your own, your native
tongue. If you have a mind, you also tell yourself that you
may be stupid, but you're not crazy. You mean to imply
that you know the difference between Oldspeak, Newspeak, and the facts. You can tell that to yourself, the
Army, and the Navy, but you can't tell it to anyone under
twenty. They don't know much, but one thing they do
know is the difference between being crazy and being stu-

pid. They are not stupid. They prefer to be crazy, and it's a wise choice.

In the looney bin of Newspeak and the same-old-jazz, the smart mind is the mind at play. The stupid mind is the one at laborious work. Serious-minded hooligans run the show and on prime time speak their minds in Newspeak. War is Peace. Peace is war in our time. Anyone over sixty can look forward to the check for cancer and the one in the mail. Anyone under twenty can look forward to the Great Society as a sick joke. Crazy they are, man: really crazy. Stupid they are not. The mind at play is grateful for The Grateful Dead.

Just over forty years ago, in a review of *Ulysses*, T. S. Eliot prepared the world with this comment:

> In using the myth, in manipulating a continuous parallel between contemporaneity and antiquity, Mr. Joyce is pursuing a method which others must pursue after him. . . . It is simply a way of controlling, of ordering, of giving a shape and a significance to the immense panorama of futility and anarchy which is contemporary history. . . . It is, I seriously believe, a step toward making the modern world possible in art.

This is the artist at work, the great mind at labor to make the world possible in art. Only a few "mad" artists suggested an alternative. The absurd art and antics of the Dadaists were accepted as proof of minds unhinged by the war. The Protestant ethic of work and salvation kept the more serious minds at work. Two decades and several wars later, however, the *unhinging* of the mind is common practice. Unhinging the mind is part of the mind at play. Would Mr. Joyce and Mr. Eliot understand the steps the younger artists are now taking? The emphasis is not to make the world possible in art, but to make life possible in the world. The challenge is greater. It has the appeal of the impossible. Crazy steps are called for, and the Watusi and the Frug are some of the steps being taken. Giant steps and all that jazz are out: little wiggles are in. Those supermen who make the world possible in art stand like museum guards at the entrance. Nor have their colossal efforts made life possible in the world. Quite the contrary. We know them by their exile. The world was what they gave up to get on with their art. That will always appeal to some artists and it will not soon go out of fashion — but there is room for more than one fashion in the world and in art. Leopold Bloom is not of much help in guiding pilgrims through the Warsaw Ghetto. Proust's remembrance of things past has not helped the living to salvage the present. There is a change in the world: to make art possible we must first live in it. Manipulating parallels and updating myths is for the birds, not for the Beatles: for minds at mindless, distracting labor, not minds at play.

For those under twenty, this is *how things are* and requires no demonstration: for those over forty the mind-at-play should be required listening. If you are not with the Beatles it is possible you are not in this world. The Beatles and their fans know how things are because they are these things. And knowing how they are, they are for love. This has puzzled and shocked those who hear only noise in their music. It is sometimes hard to hear the love for the noise, but it is there. Those over forty should be grateful. Could they say with assurance it is anywhere else? This fact has been dramatized by Beatle John Lennon, who let drop that the Beatles were more popular than Jesus. Should we be shocked or grateful? Those who love Jesus have had two thousand years to make love possible in the world. The Beatles have had five. Should we trust it to the Gallup poll? They haven't made the world *safe,* but if you're going to get crushed, let it be for love. Mr. Lennon's statement is a frank, in-group appraisal of how things really are in the battle of the sects. It's no contest. In love, if not in war, it's the Beatles all the way.

For those over forty, the doctrine of the absurd is the mind at labor, and heavy going. For those under twenty the absurd is how things are. The doctrine intuits, rather than explains, the needs of the mind for play, and the practice of non-art as the artist's way out. The new absurd task is to avoid making art of any kind. The means are improvisation, speed, and lucidity. The good *Karma*, available in the home-kit of *The Psychedelic Experience*, advises whenever in doubt, turn off your mind, relax, and float downstream. Pot is theatre. The mind upstaging its own play.

This play can be both care-free and care-full. Care-full play often reveals itself in the black humor of desperation. Synge reported on the talent for this humor among the impoverished and hope-less peasants of the Aran Islands. The hope-less and trapped sophisticate finds comfort in the purgative sick joke. The black-and-white humor of

> I don't care if it rains or freezes
> So long as I have my plastic Jee-sus

is at once both too shallow and too deep for words. The popularity of the Beatles is *vis-à-vis* this plastic Jesus. *Burn, Baby, Burn* is a recent production of Nero's fiddling while Rome burns, an all-black cast in a spectacular put on for all-white folks.

In such an admittedly dirty world, not all of the really good fun is clean. It gets worked over. It begins to look and sound unclean. The care-free world of rock 'n' roll and the care-full world of folk rock and protest undergo a change that parallels the new in-group rock and rollers. "The Jefferson Airplane," "The Lovin' Spoonful," "Mother's Little Helpers," are something more than provocative examples of the mind at play. They testify to a subversive kick openly at work. That lovin' spoonful is the Good Morning teaspoon in which the junkie cooks his fix. A player familiar with this game has an open field day with "Mother's Little Helpers." There are, indeed, many. Just what help do you have in mind? "Rainy Day Women" is a hit Bob Dylan song: a rainy day woman is a marijuana cigarette. "Straight Shooter" is a song as well as the term for the addict who takes his dope intravenously. Tunes like "Turn Me On" and "You've Got Me High" are high achievements in the art of double-talk, since they can be dug by both the in-group and the square. The folk-rock song, with its note of social protest, at once solemn, sober, and serious, proves to be the perfect media of concealment for the in-group pot luck message. This is not new. Sex and dope, two durable addictions, have often been sold over the pop song counter. But the takers were older. They were grown-up enough to be served in bars. The new double-talk is aimed at the kids who know better than to smoke in front of their parents. They buy Beatle posters. They are all for love. And they can tell you what is meant by "Norwegian Wood." Wood from Norway? That's what it means to be square.

Where pot is theatre, the music is programmed by pot luck. It is agreed, and rightly, that sex is fair game for the mind at play. The word *game* is important. It is as close, and as serious, as we care to get to the "moral" issues. The minds that play this game are expected to know it, and observe the rules. This is no longer true of the game of pot. The mind itself is the object that is played with, and there are no fast rules. For purposes of distribution, exploitation, and concealment, it has the inexhaustible resources of the language. The book and the lyrics, the words and the music, are daily made new. The suggestive vernacular of the tribe provides the junkie with both food and cover. To meet the needs of such people, to nourish minds at such play, would seem to be one of the functions of the American language. It is the essence of the game that the in-group player can take what he hears and *make* something of it. Something sexy, naturally. Something junkie, preferably. Something mysterious for the troubled, puzzled eyes of the nonplaying squares.

To pasture the mind at play, unhappily, does not preserve it from stupidities. The lovin' spoonful of freedom in the rainbow of pot involves the risk of lifelong captivity. This captivity will prove to be as *real* as the mindless, drug-given freedom elusive. The lucid improvisation of *A Hard Day's Night* is not the induced fantasies of the mind turned off. Unfortunately, it is not a distinction of much interest to players under twenty. To remain at absurd play is more important than to risk growing up.

For those growing older, but mentally still playful, there is the master-mind-at-play of James Joyce. *Finnegans Wake* will prove to be its enduring monument. Here is a word game so privately labyrinthine there is no risk involved in making it public. The essence of the game is the same for all ages: to take what you find and *make* something of it. But for the kids — as well as most of the squares — the mind of Joyce at play is still too much like work. Of absurd art, it might prove to be the most absurd. The amateur nonartist, or professional puzzlesolver, is subject to humiliation and intimidation. The scale of it is depressing. It is every inch a professional job. It lacks the ingratiatingly human amateur touch. For those under twenty, the *humor* of the situation is apt to be lost. This is best served by Pop Art, where the sick joke is both bigger and funnier than life. More important, it is good, unclean dirty fun, not just hard dirty work.

For the more sophisticated mind-at-play there is *camp*. A grown-up playground, with its paraphernalia, similar to the swings and teeter-totters of the nursery, but strictly for grown-ups. It is a joke sufficiently comprehensive to include itself. A high, see-through fence around such an arena would be recommended as part of the performance: is it there to keep initiates in, or strangers out? Of the fun games people play, camp is played by thousands who have not heard of it, unaware, up to now, how remarkably subtle some games can be. A taste for camp is a talent for solitaire. Except for Marshall McLuhan, and perhaps Hubert Humphrey, both of whom know the media and got the message, only the mind-at-play will show no surprise when the message appears on the Ed Sullivan program. It alone is undeceived as to how things are.

Great Books, Great Minds, Great Works of Art and Liberation, are part of the community of camp objects, plaster casts of heads, hands, mutilated torsos exhibited in a cemetery with lights. The Great Society is a concrete urn with the cremated ashes of our Great Expectations. Pushing out of these ashes we see Thurber-like posies and imported, ready-made *Fleurs du Mals*. They both look and smell a little silly. The scent of burning poppies cannot compare with that of burning flesh. The new growth, an Auschwitz garden of verses, cannot be classified along the lines of the old growth. One way to suggest it, if not to describe it, is to imagine that these flowers grow in reverse: that what we see sticking up in the air are the roots: what is happening is happening underground. This upside-down world more nearly corresponds to the facts of life, to the way things are. The flowers, if they're to bloom at all, must do it underground.* The crowded hothouses and museums of art, rank after centuries of cultivation, have little in common with these urns of ashes where so little seems to be happening. The pattern of this growth is the mind at play, rather than display. The disbelief in art, the distaste for taste, the need to make only the nonmade object, reflect the oversell and the imminent exhaustion of the art work as an object. It is a process, it is a happening, it is anything but an object. If they are "spontaneous" even people are art-full: in the improvised act they are artists. With a little luck life is truer than life, it is ready-made art.

The truth in this posture is that of the dance, the eloquent gesture. You can believe it or you can forget it. It is what it is: it is what it was. This playful audacity can take many forms and find all of them "liberating." For those who know how, there is nothing so liberating as play.

For those who don't know how to play, pot is theatre. In the round, the hollow round of the skull, or projected on the screen of the eyeball, the earliest and the very latest in creative, intimate cinema. *The Psychedelic Experience* advertises instant and total cinematic recall, instant and total transformation, and rebirth —

Listen:
It is almost time to return
Make the selection of your future personality according
    to the best teaching
Listen well:

For others the most available, liberating trip is the mind at play in the movies. Fellini's enchanting daymare, *Juliet of the Spirits:* Richard Lester's hard day's night with the Beatles, Antonioni's hang-up in *Blow-Up.* Its

* Mr. C. Oldenburg has recently "sculpted" a grave in Central Park.

rightness will prove its uniqueness. None other will be like it. Anything faintly like it will suffer. A perfect "happening" results in the instant cliché. There is no time (one is followed by another) for the spectator to make himself in that image. He can experience, but not possess it. The *happening* itself is elusive.

It may be premature to say that the mind at play will liquidate the cliché as an industry (the movies, the fashions, the Pop Arts, etc.) but the cookie-mold conventions of cultural history are momentarily in suspension. There isn't time. The mind at play is theatre. One dresses, speaks, and plays accordingly. To a palpable degree even nostalgia will undergo something of a sea change. It takes too long to grow a good one. Instant nostalgia is now in the works.

> O body swayed to music, O brightening glance,
> How can we know the dancer from the dance?

That is the problem that concerns us. To make such a distinction impossible. Some people *are* spontaneous — and they *are* quick and good at doing little things that are truer than life. The Beatles at madcap play are such an instance. You may be one yourself. Time will prove this to be a puzzling doctrine but for the moment it is liberating: those who dance the Watusi look with something like stupor at those who waltz. Letting go is more expressive than holding tight. For the moment that is how we feel: that is how things are. The reality that Thoreau sensed that we crave is still an illusion scaled to our talents, and momentarily our talents are with the dancer and the improvised dance.

XI: *Standard Brands and Graven Images*

Is there nothing like a Lark? No, nothing.

Not to go back to the beginning, but to go back to where we would all walk a mile for a Camel. At that time I was smoking whatever seemed to be handy. Melachrinos, Helmars, Home Runs, Luckies, and especially Dominoes at ten cents a pack. These I bought myself. They were a real man's smoke at a growing boy's price. I sent the flags in the Melachrino boxes to the girl I had left behind in Chicago, a tall, hammock-type girl who never smoked. I shifted to Helmars the summer I met Helmar, to Old Golds the winter I began to cough. I began to see through Pell Mells when they became Pall Malls. Later I met a girl who smoked Camels in the airtight flip-lid can. There was nothing to see through but the smoke. There was nothing to smoke but the fine tobacco. No flags of the world or coupons, just a real man's smoke. There's either something like a Lark, or there's nothing. Let me try and explain.

Our Tao, our way of life, calls for full exposure to standard brands, wherein we are free to make a democratic choice. Gamesmanship is achieved on seeing through the product, not the brand. Things go better with the ad than with the Coke, and they really do. Some just don't like it. Some settle for another brand. Nobody dreamed it up, nobody planned it out, at the start it was no act of cunning, foresight, or malice, it is merely what happens to children who grow up on the breakfast of champions, whose muscles and bones owe so much to Wonder Bread. An *ad*ult is a person who lives in the Ads.

In this Looking-Glass fable for moderns, the appearance is more real than the reality. It works as well as it does — and it does work well — because it has seldom, if ever, been different. It is not only *how things are*, but the way they were. It can't be helped. We are image-makers. And, *these* images are Standard Brands. The way in which they differ from Basic Illusions is both subtle and instructive. A Basic Illusion will support a grown man wide awake. A Standard Brand will support him while he sleeps. Both prove to be capable of supporting a culture and the affluence and slaughter that go along with it. So a choice exists. To be asleep or awake. The illusions of Standard Brands will not support a man with his eyes wide open, but they will shower him with pennies from heaven if he sleeps. The man who says, "I can dream, can't I?" is not awake. He is a sleeper who senses that his time capsule pill is nearing the end of its persuasion. He needs another one fast. Standard Brands offer him a wide choice.

Until recently outdoor advertising supplemented the museum of American life. A drive around the city, or a cruise around the country, provided us with blow-ups of ourselves. With TV, outdoor advertising has moved in. We live and work, using both terms loosely, in an artful surround of self-persuasion, an ambience once limited to those who could afford the comforts of press agents. On the hour we are sold on the images we have bought. No brainwashing device, no propaganda program, will compare with the willed collaboration of the American mind with advertising. When Mr. Mailer called his book *Advertisements for Myself,* his instincts, and his image, were sound. Why not? Isn't it what we all buy and sell? The Brooks Brothers shirt, the gray flannel suit, the old executive feel, the young executive look, the emblematic pack that identifies the smoker as a he-man from Marlboro country, or an Eastern chap with discriminating tastes. All but growing boys, of course, see through this nonsense: and that is how it is planned. It is how we choose — other standard brands lacking — between the men and the boys.

Image-buying is intentionally addictive: until this is true the Image hasn't *taken.* With the take it becomes a Standard Brand. This signifies that we are hosts to the virus, but strong and healthy enough to live with it. In the absence of this Image we suffer predictable withdrawal pains. We try to kill or mollify the pain by switching our brands. This is a "religious" rite in the sense that it involves idols behind altars, and the fact that anything is religious if it proves *serious* enough. A serious criminal or entertainer will soon find himself described as highly "religious," and his crime or entertaining a "religious" act. Serious theatrical moments and "religious" moments call for the same colored lights.

The Civil Rite of smoking acquired religious status when it was seriously related to cancer. So we were living after all, burning the candle at both ends! Short-term faddists of personal survival periodically threaten this national Image, but both the public and the advertisers recognize its importance to the nation. So we may lose a percentage of smokers? A calculated risk. It lies beyond calculation what would happen if Americans refused to smoke. Both the public will and the public *image* have proved to be stronger than the threat of cancer: the temporary withdrawal reassures the addict of the importance of his addiction. On the heels of every *scare* the sales zoom up. We have an *image* to maintain. It costs us more than the smoke. To complain about this is a typical example of irrelevant consumer research. Who cares about the tobacco? For years now we've been smoking filter tips.

What's new makes its debut, and receives our blessings, in the theatre of advertising. The newest thing in our lives of importance is prime time. As part of our affluence it follows on prime rib, and on its appearance required no explanation. We *knew*. In one way or another we always know. Such a phrase testifies to the durable and coherent elements of our culture, and the continued vitality of the language we have at our disposal. *Prime time.* Who makes it prime? You and me. *Prime* is what it is made in our *image*, and our image is getting expensive. It takes dough. Prime time is time-is-money brought up to date. Money is time. Really good money is prime time.

Three or four hours of really prime time might produce an image that would last forever — or almost. This image is printed where ordinary wear and tear, time and tide, won't touch it. Impossible to erase. Only *another* image will take its place. This indelible image is printed on what we call the mind's eye. To that extent it's tricky. But the sure way of doing it is prime time.

Take the images we have. Did you note a blurring, as if someone jarred the camera, when CBS took over the

Yankees? I once felt pretty personal about the Yankees. I had, as we say, an investment in them. For many years I had the pocket to a pair of Babe Ruth's barnstorming pants. I mention this to emphasize that a certain amount of my own prime time went into the Yanks. I felt a loss of time, so to speak, when they suddenly changed their image. That's a small-time response to big changes in prime time.

Just a few months later RCA announced a barrier-breaking merger with Random House, a publisher of books. This was hailed, and rightly, as a breakthrough in the field of *communications*. Communications, like prime time, is relatively new. That is to say, its *image* is still forming. People have heard a lot about it, but they aren't sure what it is. But soon they will be. Communications *is* prime time. If it's prime, it's communicating.

A prime example of communication is the way this new image is catching on. Take United Artists and Consolidated Foods. The old image was movies, stars, and canned goods. That one is out. The new image, as described by the spokesman for Consolidated Foods, is "a major entry into the broad and rapidly expanding field of entertainment and mass communications." Food, football, and the news share the prime time with Bob Hope. What on first glance seems a little strange — or as the headline commented, *Strange Bedfellows* — after a moment's reflection proves to be a natural breakthrough: Artists and Foods, the Compleat Inner and Outer Man. It is the very nature of communications to eliminate outmoded distinctions. Beer is baseball, hair oil is football, tired blood is the news. With the late show, quick relief and a choice of pain.

Custom decrees there is something called a World of Sports. It is a question of accent. The sports are in the bleachers, or home with a beer watching prime time. Both worlds of sports are part of the empire of communications. The prime-time sportster is learning not to keep his eye on the ball. If he did he would miss the overall message of communications. The game is played, stopped, started, or prolonged according to the ground rules of the sponsor. The color of the ice, the color of the grass, and the color of the players, are elements to be orchestrated in the overall, living world of color. The important detail is how it will look, or hang, in your room. At what hour, on what night or day you are sure to be there.

The relevance of such details came to the game with the phenomenon of the bonus-baby. The game is not the thing, or one baby is not worth the price of a dozen. The sums offered to young men with a knack for hitting, throwing, catching, putting, or running with balls of various sizes, is not so much a reflection on their talents as it is an index to their sponsors. What the sponsor is selling, cash-on-the-line, is prime time.

If the camera is speeded up in the manner that shows us flowers opening and closing, the actual living and dying face of nature, we would have no sure way of knowing if Arnold Palmer is a golfer or a corporation. These two aspects of the athlete would merge. It is the first of the new image-mergers of prime time. It is not clear, at the moment, which of the images might have the longer life. What game, after all, is the one he is paid the most to play?

All of the big name stars must face this dilemma of eventually merging with the product, or products, the metamorphosis of the Image into the Standard Brand. The policy of endorsement, with its modest beginnings in tonic water, liver pills, baseballs, and bats, has been enlarged and transformed into an industry of appropriation. The product, *any* product, appropriates the name. The name Arnold Palmer need not be confined to golf balls, clubs, and golf paraphernalia. Ted Williams, a baseball Immortal, has given his endorsement to most of the products that might come to the hand, ear, or eye of a Sportsman — the Sportsman being anybody with money and leisure. The *World* of sports thus becomes the world of *Sports*. It will soon be difficult to imagine a product a sports image might not endorse, or an enterprise so strange he cannot identify or merge with it. Real estate, hard and soft drinks, hard and soft ware, cars, batteries and tires, shop tools, Hi-fi (it is better for the athlete to bypass the kitchen), hair oils, foot powders, Supp-Hose, firearms (the gun will merge with *any* Sports image) — the instant transfer of the *image* is now accepted American practice. Called to the purchaser's attention, he would ask, "Why not?" It makes the athlete a fast buck, and the buyer a better sportsman. Both images are "improved."

An image currently in need of much improvement is the image of war. I was recently watching war with Huntley & Brinkley, on prime time. Selling the war is the same as prosecuting the war. So I was properly amazed to see the war slipped off on a siding in western Kansas to let the Capote Cold Blood express roar through to Holcomb. For two or three minutes, that is, Capote had higher billing than Vietnam. On the exchange, Cold Blood went up as the war went down. Both were news, and at that precise moment both were advertising on prime time. That is stranger, in its way, than the murder he reported, or what the author referred to as new fiction. No fiction is so strange as what we see nightly on prime time.

The notorious discrepancy between the war and the facts as reported by Secretary McNamara is the *typical* discrepancy between the product and its advertising. Mc-

Namara must *sell* the war in order to prosecute it. We are asked to buy the war on the basis of his performance. If it goes well, it's a *good* war — it conforms, that is, to the advertising. If it goes bad, it needs a *new* image, and fast. The blurring image at the center of this mural is the image of LBJ. As the war goes, so goes the image. A war of nerves is best described as a war of images. It is a bad one if it slips on the Gallup poll. After prime-time appearances over one weekend, each calculated to reinforce the *old* image, the headlines of the morning paper read —

BIG JUMP IN JOHNSON POPULARITY

The proper word is image. A big jump in the image, thanks to prime time. This is true of General Motors, General Foods, General Electric, and Vietnam. If the image is good it pays to advertise. If the image is bad you need a new press agent. People are made by fools like you and me, but only prime time can make an image. Anyhow, that's the gospel. You can ignore it at your own risk.

Nobody dreamed it all up, nobody planned it all out, it is no act of foresight and no deed of hindsight, it is merely what happens when things are the way they are. It's just that simple. It's just that inscrutably complex. You may think there's something like a Lark, but there isn't. Not on prime time. And there's nothing, anywhere, like Marlboro country, or the strength of Ajax, or the wonders of Bayer, or how glad you really are you used Dial. No, there's nothing like it. The image has long ago outdistanced the thing itself.

XII: *The Sound of One Hand Clapping*

The sound of one hand clapping? I once heard and saw it with my own eyes, in the crowded Christmas aisles of a department store. On the floor the slippery film of mush tracked in from the street. A gentleman and his consort, both elderly, stood at a counter piled with hand-bags: the gentleman's hat, the lady's fur piece powdered with yuletide snow. What caught my eye? His bowler. I have always admired bowlers. Elegance, breeding, snob-bery, enchanting bygone things. His gaze seemed inward; from one arm an umbrella dangled. He wore rubbers and spats. As I gazed he raised the arm on which the umbrella was hooked, fingered the brim of the hat, then tipped it as if greeting a lady. At this precise moment his free gloved hand slipped between the bowler and his head, tapped the bald crown thrice, as you would a child, then dropped to his side. So what? We all fiddle a bit with our extremities.

We pull noses, pluck at ears, pry at warts and moles, stroke or pick at chins, tirelessly swipe down wisps or licks of hair, and scratch or probe anything within reach. So what is a little rhythmic pat on the skull?

What is it? The sound of one hand clapping. I heard it. So did his wife. Without turning from her screening of the handbag counter she reached back a hand, trained by years of experience, and gripped the wrist of the arm he had raised, lowered it to his side. This served as a lever to return the bowler to his head. She then released the hand, using both of her own to open the zipper of a handbag. Once more his left hand, the umbrella rocking, went up to courteously tip the hat, and his free, gloved hand slipped into the opening as into a drawer, thrice tapped his head. Preoccupied, she let it go on through one, two, three series of tappings, each pat-pat-pat. Once more, as if taking the hand of a child from an unbecoming position, her hand went back, found what it sought, lowered the hand to his side. His bowler returned to its proper place on his head. For a moment only: then once more, as the coin dropped and the levers operated, his left hand began its ascent toward his hat — but the movement of the gears was audible to her. If one is trained, and has good ears, one hears the sign flip up that precedes the applause. She heard it, turned quickly from the counter to interrupt the gesture, adjust the folds of his muffler, then place into his free hand the strap of her heavy handbag, weighting his arm to the floor. That did it. That stopped the sound of the one hand clapping, but not the internal movement and strain of the gears. When she retrieved her bag the one-hand clapping would resume.

It may do violence to the mysterious East to suggest we are a nation of one-hand clappers. With one hand we applaud, with the other we grope to put an end to a mechanical reflex. It is the laugh machine that has the last laugh. In the applause reflex we have the ultimate refinement in audience participation, the perfection of self-help in the delicate operation of brainwashing. The laugh machine is a convenience, but not a necessity. We are a well-trained people. We no longer need the cue to laugh and applaud.

As Americans we choose to gloss history as a record of privileged abuses, with America the lyrical passage that sets men free. Up till now we have given little or no consideration to the arts of self-abuse. The concept is not congenial. We prefer to believe that such a person is *sick*. The lusty proliferation of the sick has faced us with new and staggering problems, but better the problem than admit to the self-abuse. Willy Loman is prepared to admit that a salesman's life is hell, but not that in *buying* what he sold, he killed himself. The triumph of advertising, creative advertising, is in Willy Loman's unshaken belief in self-abuse as a way of life. He died a true believer. He believed to the last that was the way things were. So long as we can buy — and sell — we are stoically resigned to our fate.

In the personal column of the San Francisco *Chronicle* is the appeal of a man better off dead. That is what he says:

> HEART ATTACK VICTIM — Would have been better off dead. Am unable to obtain life and health insurance at anything near reasonable premiums. Want to contact others in same predicament to discuss ways of solving problem.

These few words speak louder than a thousand pictures. This victim's fate worse than death is to live without the proper insurance. All he asks from life is reasonable premiums. In the pursuit of this ideal, this vision of the good life, he would like nothing more than to contact others in the same predicament — who, like him, would otherwise surely be better off dead. This unsolicited testimonial is similar to the statements of those we consider brainwashed, and speaks out boldly, and frankly, of the joys of captivity. Indoctrination has achieved its ends when the doctrine is accepted as the way things are, part of our carefree way of life.

The man who advertises his faith has not lost faith in advertising. That he should be worth more dead than alive is a commonplace fact that he shares with many others. An American Tragedy, in this context, is the man who dies uninsured, or the man who cannot obtain, while still alive, reasonable premiums. In this context tragedy, the tragic condition, is a social disease from which too many suffer until it is conquered by technology or insurance. The *painless* tragedy is a current practice in the use of drugs to minimize shock. The proper insurance policy is the ideal long-term therapy. The check that arrives from a reputable source, symbolized by Greek columns or the rock of Gibraltar, brings spiritual as well as practical consolations. One is in good *hands*. In the advertisement we see them, the hands of God, tenderly cupping our widening world of possessions, the car, the house and furnishings, the mortgage, the carefree future of the loved ones, the education of the young ones, the care of the old ones, and the respectful removal of the dead ones, all in one package, one premium, and one policy. What *faith* has promised and delivered so much? The policy is democratic, honoring alike the good and the bad, the idle and loutish, regardless of race, color, caste, or creed, so long as the premiums are paid up. In all but one small detail it is superior to anything bought and sold in the past: there are no losses. No, every loss is a gain. Anything we can assess can be redeemed in dollars and cents. This remarkable service confronts the benefactor, hereinafter known as the beneficiary, with the only loss not covered by the policy. How describe it? If we could, surely Lloyd's of London would insure it. The loss of loss. Somehow related to the gain of life. It is hard to describe, to make it as real as our other, tangible possessions, so often taken from us, as the policy says, by the actions of wind, earth, fire, and water, or an act of God. The loss of loss is not new. It was what we once described as tragic. Irredeemable. The like of something, all in all, we shall not know again. Is it possible this loss — not the one prescribed by law or insurance, accident or design — is the one that requires the use of humane pain-killers that make life supportable? Is it for the loss — or that we cannot lose — that we would rather not weep? For an answer to these and other questions we can look into ourselves, at uninsured risks, or wait to find them in the small print in the next inclusive one-package policy.

Audience participation is at its most advanced in the advantages of "group insurance," where the numbers game pays insured dividends. A programmed life and death, based on a statistically sound and computed image, assures the participant there is no loss without a gain. A side effect, or rather group dividend, is the expansion of group consciousness as the individual consciousness sensibly withers. This sensation is accompanied by relief. The patient's response is that a load has been taken off his back. Responsibilities, the whole destructive package, are covered by one payment and shared by the group. Relief of this sort is also supplied by the "family management" organizations, who take care of our numerous, confusing obligations, and send us just one, plain sensible bill — plus a charge for this service. These benefits are real, another service we pay for, and contribute to a new — or very old — state of mind. It is the group mind, or consciousness, from which the individual consciousness so hesitantly, so painfully, and so inadvisedly emerged. The fire is at one's back, a single shadow darkens the jungle ahead. The re-emergence of group consciousness will find its expression in sighs of relief. This shift of the square peg to the square was signaled by a memorable and telling expression: "I've had it." These words express in a private sense what *Going Out of Business* expresses publicly. The first-person pronoun has been going out of business in our public life. The parallel sentiment today would be expressed as "We've had it!", a suitable caption for the Great Society. Such a shift of consciousness is not unheard of, but its thoroughness is cause for wonder. Behavior that strikes some of us as mighty peculiar is merely evidence of the emerging new order. This behavior involves the concept of privacy. It is widely assumed that all human beings have it, and if they don't have it, passionately want it. A private life has been the goal of American life. We are aware that privacy is under attack by magazine photographers and fiendishly ingenious gadgets, but we prefer to ignore the fact that privacy has become more intolerable than exposure. It is privacy that millions cannot bear. The conclusive experiment in this transformation is one recently conducted under controlled laboratory conditions. What is a controlled experiment? One that excludes privacy. One that contributes to "the general good."

This experiment was widely hailed and covered in the nation's press. My own clipping reads: A Clinical Report on Sex Activity. It concerns an eleven-year inquiry (would nine or fifteen have modified it?) into the physiology of sex (the psychology we have already had) published under the title *Human Sexual Response*.

The inquiry involved the direct observation of 382 women and 312 men as they engaged in sexual acts. The authors wrote the book because they consider the sexual performance an "integral part of sexuality," and sexuality "a dimension and an expression of personality." This remarkable statement is in the Newspeak of social science, and quite simply defies commentary. If there are human beings who do not consider sexual performance a part of sexuality, what can one do? My interest in the experiment, however, lies in the 382 volunteer women, and the 312 volunteer men. The discrepancy gives the men the edge, until one learns the range of the age groups participating. One of the gentleman was eighty-nine. One of the ladies seventy-eight. They were not spied on. They were not compelled to be human guinea pigs as in the Nazi experiments. No, they volunteered. They did it all for science and the general good.

Allowing for the deviate and pathological types that would stampede to be part of such an experiment, the turnout testifies to a shift in what is considered normal behavior. This shift is away from the private act. What good is it? Who has seen it? What a pity so few share it. In withdrawing into privacy one withdraws from the group. If there is something to be *gained* by doing it in public — then all should gain. All these people were *adults*, as we loosely define them; not children in a state of nature, but people who have been shaped, and misshaped, by American life. What do they tell us? They tell us that privacy is a thing of the past. That the cameraman and the ingenious gadgets merely take over what we have relinquished. The picture window is to be looked into, rather than out of.

The new wave, of which this is a lap, has for some time

been the new thing for the intellectual, the sophisticate, and the artist, who once found in privacy the lineaments of the last frontier. The liquidation of privacy is all that is left. As the artist takes this frontier by storm, stimulating, among the initiate, the excitement of a campus panty raid, the message gets through to the unsophisticated as painlessly and as profoundly as fallout. They need only read the papers. They stand in line to volunteer at the laboratory. If the door is opened by a man in white they are in good hands.

What they bring to this experiment is a burden that has temporarily lost its meaning — the nature of individual life. The center of this life was privacy. They are willing and eager to exchange this life, with its loneliness, burdens, and frustrations, for the open-air, open-ended, open-minded life of shared experience, the meaning and the value lying in that it is shared, rather than what it is. A limit has been found to private effort, private dreams, and private life.

From the splintered woodwork of the American scene the last of the tribe is now appearing; town and hillbillies, living fossils, dragged off the reservation or flushed and baited into the open by Medicare, Sexicare, Hearticare, and Headicare. Under the new dispensation they are all listed as beneficiaries.

The younger rebels have causes, the older rebels have kids, the senior citizens have a brighter outlook, and I have this memory of a baseball game between the Yankees and the White Sox. Who won it? I've forgotten. It's another detail I remember. In the last inning an announcement was made over the public address system. A record had been broken. The record broken was that of the paid attendance to all home games played on Tuesday. There was a wave of applause. The two men seated beside me rose and cheered. I did not cheer and applaud (my mouth was full of popcorn) but I marveled. That sunny, record-breaking afternoon I witnessed the end of one game and the beginning of another. The game of one-hand clapping. The record-breaking sport any number can play. The laugh machine laughs, the applause machine applauds, audience participation daily sets new records, and the sound of one hand clapping can be heard the length and breadth of the land.

XIII: *Some Other Country*

> My lawyer friend told me at once that I was
> evidently in such a mess that he thought
> the best thing I could do was to become a
> citizen of some other country.
>
> EDMUND WILSON

In his book *The Cold War and the Income Tax:
A Protest,* Edmund Wilson's candor matches his indignation. "It may seem naïve," he writes, "and even stupid, on
the part of one who had worked for years on a journal
which specialized in public affairs, that he should have
paid so little attention to recent changes in the income tax
laws; . . ." This statement suggestively defines the mess
Mr. Wilson got himself into. Naïveté — some would say
stupidity — concerning changes in the income tax laws.
The mess was such that he was legally advised to become
the citizen of some other country.

But there are many other countries. Which one did he
have in mind? On this crucial point Mr. Wilson's legal advice is vague. One gathers it is *any* other country more
predictable in its tax laws. A country where naïveté in
this matter is not considered a federal crime. A country

where it is admitted that an intellectual has other things on his mind than tax laws. Mr. Wilson's protest is in the name of all men who admit to a higher calling. It often finds them naïve, it sometimes makes them stupid, but that is one of the risks. When they stick to *their* country we call them intellectuals — when they wander far afield we call them eggheads. In either case, the other country is the one without the mess. Mr. Wilson's protest is for those, like himself, who so often seem to be men without a country. While putting up with the shortcomings of the one in which they live, they have their mind's eye firmly on the other, a country where Truth, Freedom, Art, and flexible tax laws prevail. When Mr. Wilson filed his protest, rather than his return, it was with the implicit understanding that he shared this frailty with the reader, a naïve, possibly stupid, but well-meaning egghead like himself.

The grain of what we call the American mind, over which thought passes with a rasping lisp, is peculiarly unsympathetic to the man who thinks. It is hardly necessary to add *just* thinks. A thinking man, Adlai Stevenson, went against this grain skillfully, and with patience, but it was his charm that won us over, not his thought. The very absurdity of his undertaking aroused our grudging admiration. When he didn't seem to learn better, his persistence stirred our compassion. This chronic situation finally found its resolution in putting him to pasture in the United Nations. It was generally agreed that the thing for him to do was become the citizen of some other country, a place for those who are so often victimized by their own ideals.

A veiled contempt for the man who merely thinks is natural to the thinkers we admire. Thoreau is at pains to control his distaste for the pundits of Emerson's circle, a vortex of thought that still spins the academic heads. The

sheer per capita volume of transcendental thought, accumulated by starlight, recorded by lamplight, ventilated
and distributed by daylight, might well prove to exceed
any other home-grown, nineteenth-century product. The
issues were crucial. Men in relative darkness seeking for
light. It is hardly a whim of fate that Thomas Alva Edison
came up with the solution. Not the rosy, heartwarming
flow of talk, nor the gemlike flame of art. Practical. A
small glass bulb that gave off light. Mr. McLuhan aptly
describes it as "pure information." This remarkable
method of dispensing with darkness reduced the voltage
of abstract thought. A *practical* solution to abstract problems was possible. This sensible, no-nonsense approach to
thought was natural to a people who started from scratch.
Ben Franklin pioneered and exploited this opening. Numberless inventive and ingenious Yankees schooled themselves in their own kitchens. Thoreau, Whitman, Edison,
and Mark Twain would have found talk more congenial,
the time more profitably spent, if while the tongues
wagged, their hands were also busy shelling peas, shining
a boot, trimming a wick, the background humming with
the sound of women preparing a meal. Something new in
a participating environment.

The extreme polarities of the American mind, transcendental visions and practical gadgets, in this milieu
were nurtured simultaneously. It is the gadgets, however,
that have conquered the world. It is gadgets that Americans buy and sell. It cannot be ruled out that a remarkable
gadget, continuing the researches begun by Franklin, will
one day transcend the nature of the data-fodder that men
feed it. Stranger things have happened. Strange happenings are in the American grain. Dissatisfaction with
thinking, as well as mere thinkers, satisfaction with
gadgets that dispense with darkness, prepares the way for

the feedback circuit that will dispense with thought, if not tax problems. We like things that work. To think mere thoughts is to be unemployed.

Of our rapidly diminishing natural resources one remains inexhaustible: our genius for coining the memorable word or phrase for things we do not like. We are not without talent in other departments, but our instinct for abuse is something special. The word *egghead* combines grassroots with universal and instant communication. In a single, lucidly suggestive term, we express our inexhaustible contempt. The label also sticks. Nothing on the market will wash it off. The scarlet letter, the four-letter word, plus a variety of blemishes too numerous to mention, all have their appropriate antidote or balm in the family medicine cabinet. But not egghead. Anyone so labeled must resign himself to his condition. His life and times as an egghead constitute his store of raw material. If a novelist, he writes protest novels; if a painter he paints protest paintings; if he is a critic and scholar like Mr. Wilson he writes, quite simply, a *protest* — padding it out, to make a book of it, with some random observations on war and taxes. They are durable subjects. Both egg and non-egghead give them considerable thought.

At a somewhat late date, for a man of his experience, Mr. Wilson's scholarly eye discovered home-grown bureaucracy. He knew such things existed in bureaucratic countries, the largest of which he had given much study, but he had not, as he says, imagined such things existed right under his nose. Mr. Wilson's lawyer, a friend and Princeton classmate, a man who could think if not a *mere* thinker, was struck speechless when he learned in what country Mr. Wilson believed himself to be living. Although old friends, and good Princeton men, they were apparently living in unrelated worlds. At the end of his undoubted harassment and torment Mr. Wilson could concur in the lawyer's judgment: a man in such a horrible mess should find himself another country and go live in it. This one, with its cold war and its tax laws, was not for him. "I have always thought myself patriotic and have been in the habit in the past of favorably contrasting the United States and the Soviet Union: but . . . I have finally come to feel that this country, whether or not I continue to live in it, is no longer the place for me."

This statement testifies — more than his problems with the tax laws — that Mr. Wilson has been living in a country of his choosing all this time. So have many others. A country more to the taste of the persecuted egghead is now a thriving part of the American landscape. It may well be superior to any similar preserves available in the past. The Custom House, the foreign service, the enlightened patron, are welcome but sportively fickle windfalls in the life of the artist and the intellectual. The new country makes room for them within the legal boundaries of the old one. When we enter the precincts of the Campus City we still assume it is an inner sanctum, an urban annex of the Groves of Academe. When we think of the campus, perhaps we still think of the Ivy League. In such archives we buried our past and we do not want the remains molested. But for some years now the closed campus has been the site of a new Open City, where the egghead, the rebel, and the slumming square have set up operations. The modern ivory tower gleams less with ivory than the sun resplendent on a field of placards, the shaven lawns given over to hosts of unshaven beats. The controversial figure, the rebellious scholar, the novelist, the poet, and the painter now apply for mortgages, tenure, and take up residence in the Campus City. Is it some other country?

The neo-Gothic, neo-Greek, Tudor, Colonial, old Mediterranean, and Industrial Park Modern, the source of so much egghead abuse and inexhaustible square nostalgia, now supply an appropriately foreign setting for the seasonal flood of transient students, no small number trying the campus on for color and size. There may or may not be a gate, an archway, or a plaque, announcing that this is hallowed ground, and there may or may not be grackels nesting in the ivy. If they exist it is a last reminder that this city was once a closed one, a sanctuary of special interests and privileges. No walls surround it. They would obstruct the flow of traffic and the predictable expansion. A free or paid-way may fence it on one side, a slum or a housing tract on the other. It hardly matters. In a few weeks or months one will be torn down, another put up.

From the road the Campus City resembles an industrial park humming with wartime orders. Lights burn at night. There are acres and acres of scooters and cars. This impression is accurate in that it is a plant that turns out a product. It is also a mausoleum that preserves the past. The structures may be high-rise, low-rise, or subterranean, they might prove to be old or shamelessly new as barracks. The walks are of asphalt. The transplanted trees are leashed to the ground. The boundaries of the city are clearly defined by a belt of bumper-to-bumper parking. This flexible chain has replaced the wall, and suggests the major change in the city limits. There are none. At night the campus citizens crawl back into the surrounding woodwork. It is more a matter of real estate than custom.

Entrance to the Campus City is possible wherever the lights bring the traffic to a stop. It is there that the squares, snug in their cockpits, peer through their tinted windshields at the passing frieze of eggheads, shaven and unshaven, clad and unclad, but within the city precincts respectably housed. The best is none too good. We want our children — and our old folks — to have the best. Those who march in tandem past the captive horde of squares seem to bear no greater burden than the hair on their heads, the placards under their arms. Five days of the week the citizens of the slave world confront those of the free world at these stop lights. Girls shapely and dumb, unshapely and smart, young and elderly matrons, married and unmarried couples, schoolboys and idlers, delinquents and scholars, housewives, trailer-wives, exchanged wives, swapped wives, drop-ins, drop-outs, presentable, lamentable, normal, abnormal, reborn, foreign born, stillborn, unborn, an endless animated frieze ornamented with colorful, doleful, beggarly, and elegant clumps of hippies, a medieval assembly appropriate to this new medieval city. Diverse, inverse, multiverse, and perverse: nutty as a fruit cake, moth-eaten as a tapestry, casual, mannered, preposterous, and presumptuous at a glance. Also moving, occasionally inspiring, a pilgrimage to Delos, to Selma, to Olympus, a Children's Crusade with senior citizen support, a *Voyage au Bonheur,* a night and daymare of illusion more disturbing than dreams, more addictive than dope. INCIPIT VITA NOVA. Here begins a new life. Like the gate or the archway that once marked the entrance, this chiseled inscription is now missing, but it is what one reads on the brows of the addicted and between the lines scrawled on the placards. A new life. God knows where it will end, but here it begins.

An impalpable line defines the boundaries, but not the air. One may find it like that breathed through the lips of beach girls who have been carefully trained to rescue the

drowning, rhythmically bending to the beach-wrecked victim with the kiss of life. Another may find it thin, or air-
conditioned, an artificial climate that weakens the muscles, softens the mind. In either case, those accustomed to
this climate are soon addicted to it. They feel at home in
it. They may never feel so comfortable anywhere else. The
change most difficult to describe, yet felt the most profoundly, is that the center of the world has shifted. The
real world, of course. The one once presumed to be *out
there*. Now — if one can trust one's feelings — it is *in
here*. Many feel they have known this from the beginning.
The world of heart's desire, of Love, Joy, Truth, and Jus-
tice, frustrated and doomed by the world *out there*, is the
world in here. This fundamental intuition, this inalienable *right*, the Campus City gives authority and substance.
The landscape of the heart is right there on the map.
Within its confines a civilized order has replaced the tooth
and claw of the outside jungle. This is not new — but it
is new to believe that the center of the real world has
shifted, and that the Campus City lies at the heart of it. At
any given moment more than six million citizens give
flesh and substance to this illusion. The unreal city is the
one that still rises, on the hour, with the suburban Bab-
bitts, who daily stream by the Campus City on their way to
the towers of Zenith. Neither the sons of Babbitt, nor his
wife and daughters, turn to the Campus City for distraction and refuge. Quite the contrary: the campus is now
where the action is. At its rim one finds the portable barricades. It is open alike to rebels, hippies, eggheads, flat-
heads, and squares on safari. Something in the air, or in
the smoke-dimmed cafeteria lighting, harmonizes the
elements that would be insupportable elsewhere. The
young man with the beard, the lank, unwashed hair, the
sockless feet in the stirrup heel boots, listens to the ma-

tron's (back for her Master's) respectable view of Camus, Genet, or Vietnam. At home he would hoot. Here he ponders and puffs his pipe. When he leaves she turns and says to her companion, "They certainly go the whole route, don't they?"

The whole route. That is what one finds assembled in the campus cafeteria. It is a better place to study the route than on the map. The light, smoke, and endless movement of the traffic is similar to a cafe in an over-crowded airport. You may, or may not, stumble on your present companion again. The variety and appearance of the assembled pilgrims inclines toward the medieval. Artisans abound. Bearded and barefooted figures of saintly aspect are not missing. If there is a missing detail of importance it is the smell of food. Both the coffee and the food are prepared and designed to give off no smell. Odorless, the coffee steams in the cup the poet stirs with a tongue depresser. Spoons are in shortage. The citizens have appropriated most of the spoons. There is also a chronic shortage of sugar dispensers and salt and pepper shakers. They disappear. The citizen of the Campus City has a casual attitude toward objects. He takes them for granted. He also takes many of them home. Experience has assured him that there are more wherever they came from. That is a law: one of the few he has learned to trust. Although turnstiles are absent at the gates to the city, the doors to buildings and classrooms, they will be found, with an attendant, wherever crucial materials are stock-piled. The library provides only a temporary shelter for many books. It is felt that such things are on the house, and this is one's house. It is considered *existential* to cop whatever one might really use.

The cafeteria is where the Campus City celebrates it-self. A covered piazza, odorous and fraternal with the exhumations of the natives, who huddle in corners, like bandits, or form ad hoc committees, or spoon or slurp up food while reading, or smoke, or flirt, or rest their heads on piles of books or cyclist helmets, cooling their minds before the drag race of a test. A table of ten are silent while they listen to the trial run of a preach-in. The statement is read like a manifesto by a boy with a face like Savonarola. A giant with Rasputin's beard, his own nose, a face divided into uneven portions, goes by with a bowl of chili and a carton of orange drink. Locks of unwashed hair sweep his shoulders. He wears a Chinese red beret. Pressed to his left side is a placard that reads MAKE LOVE NOT WAR. He also sports a buckle of Mexican silver and limps from an afternoon session of karate. If they crossed this room Sancho Panza and Quixote would arouse little comment, all of it favorable. But the Secretary of State, with his satchel-bearing aides, would look stranger than Marco Polo. But not peculiar. The city is also open to squares. These bizarre ingredients meet and mingle in the blender of the Campus City, an existential stage where the amateur plays out his role. The feature of this performance, renewed daily, is that the intended audience is absent. It is understood by all, unstated but implicit, that the real audience — if not the world — is *out there*. The on-campus performance is the off-Broadway production that one day, hopefully soon, will hit the high road, bringing the brave new world to the eroding world of squares. Both the campus citizen and the outside square share the knowledge that each lives in some other country. The feeling is mutual that the other country is unreal.

In the last decade the immediate present has inundated the majority of big campus cities. Silt from this deposit, enriched yearly, now thickens on the floors of the abandoned archives. Some corridors are temporarily blocked.

Others are kept open, at considerable expense, just for the hell of it. The exceptional citizen, with perhaps increased interest, will continue his perverse and solitary diggings, but for the majority of the new arrivals the inundation will interest them more than the archives. They are part of it. They contribute to it. The delta of silt is their proper subject. Representative deposits of this spreading delta provide the students with their subject matter.

The immediate present has its literature, its art, its science, its politics, and its apologists. What else *is* there? The question goes unanswered in the Campus City. Others are both more relevant and pressing. The immediate present is increasingly sufficient unto itself. The past is what one finds discarded in the attic, or served up live on a major cruise: picturesque, oversold, obsolete. Just recently this past was a bottomless well fed by inexhaustible springs of data. The bucket now scrapes the bottom. The inexhaustible data rains from space. Daily, on the hour, there is more of it, rather than less. The planet earth is a small piece of data in this larger dispensation.

Although the role of the past has not been publicly questioned, and its monuments stand in the flooded forum, it is privately a topic that has come up too late to discuss. The relevant past is where we were this morning. It is what we are making at any given moment. The immediate present is as much of the past as we need to survive. What's old? Whatever just a moment ago was new. The future is a wide-screen cineramic production into which we are absorbed during the performance. We shoot the chutes: we circle the world in so and so many hours. The curvature of space is the horizon that sweeps around us. Past, present, and future constitute a single *happening*. The apparent gap between the moonbound rocket and the earthbound hippie proves to be an optical illusion.

Both are in orbit. Both are relatively free of the gravity drag of the past. If you can't take it with you, why take it? Fewer and fewer do. Lawrence's poetry of the immediate present, imperfect, unconsummated and unfinished, may prove to be but a cunning disguise for the past essential to man's survival. The past within us. The "trip" embedded in the cube of sugar. A very old story, an even older illusion, before it is a new one. How to live, how to love, how to swing, and how to orbit are time-worn games. The action is wherever these questions, and these games, get a suitable airing. The answers vary: the action of the game is answer enough. The Campus City provides the space and the open forum, and the games that are played provide the answers. Here and now.

It is this day that dawns, the smog permitting, on the silted greens of our campus cities, where the immediate present threatens to inundate the established past. It has been so long in coming, and so quick in ascendance, that most of us have failed to recognize it: some of us have been living in some other country for sometime. Naïveté — some would say stupidity — has distracted the rebel, the egghead, and the square from the brave new world right in our midst. That it hath such people in it we have no one to thank but ourselves.

XIV: *The Rat, the Cat, the Warsaw Ghetto, and Paul*

He is a neighbor's child, three years, four months, and some days old. His name is Paul. If I say rat he says *rad*, if I say cat he says *cad*, but if I say Paul he says absolutely nothing. He turns and runs. His sister is slender, small-boned, very pretty and civilized. He is a fat, oozing blob and uncivilized. He likes to break things. He likes to lift cats by their tails. We have a cat without a tail and that explains his interest in us. His mother says he is *just* like his father, which means he knows what he wants and it's not Castoria. In the morning what he wants is to lift cats by their tails and carry the mail.

Every morning his pretty sister walks him down the driveway to the mailboxes. All the boxes, fortunately, are on posts too high for Paul to reach them. He has tried. In the wool of his red sweater are the redwood splinters from our post. When his sister takes the mail from the box he bawls like a calf until she gives it to him. Why does he want it? He can't read it. He has tried but found that he can't eat it. Five out of the six days of the week it is circulars. But it is something that his sister does every morning and Paul is determined that *he* will do it. Why he does it he will learn about later. A very small detail. The big detail is to do what is being done and think about why you did it later. In his mother's opinion Paul is very advanced for his age.

I am fifty-six years, eight months, and two weeks, and in the opinion of my wife not advanced for my age. However, when I go for the mail I can reach it myself. It's the one advantage I have over Paul. Most of my mail, like his, is circulars, but he has the advantage that he can't read it. It all looks smashing to him. I can tell by his clutch. When I read a circular I sometimes stand there as if lost in thought about what it tells me. In a way I am. It *is* accurate to say I am lost in thought. I stand there in a wood of my own thinking and I have not as yet found my way out. I did not even have to discover for myself what my trouble is, since the language tells me. Lost in thought. One day I heard it, or read it somewhere, and knew that I was. One day Paul, who is advanced for his age, will have a similar experience, and his mother will think, "What a child I have made! He is lost in thought!" Like all mothers she will be right. Paul and I are lost in thought together. More than fifty-three years separate us but we are both lost in thought about the future. He, when he looks at me. I, when I look at him. I am plainly the more wide-eyed and lost because he *is* the future in a way that escapes me. I shall never know what he knows, or be lost in thought the way he will be lost. What will not be found in books, in space, in dreams, in prophecies, and programs will be found in Paul. He is plump. He is headstrong. He very

likely has a touch of arteriosclerosis. He is tireless, shame-
less, relatively mindless, incurably willful about the mail.
Never mind what the mail is about. That can wait. That
is what we have been doing for centuries and one of the
passions that binds us together. In a remarkable way Paul
and I are lost in the same thought.

In a dim but palpable way I sensed that while watching
a documentary on TV, *The Frontiers of the Mind.* The first
thing I thought of was Paul. Every hour or so, according to
his mother, he opened a new frontier. Zipped into his play-
suit, in a helmet with ear muffs, he resembles something
new in a spacebrat. Too new for the cats. At the sight of
him they are gone for hours. If they are not gone, he tries
to pick one up by the tail. "No! No!" I say to Paul. "Bad!
Bad!"

"Bat, bat," he says, and claps his mittens.

"Driveway is bad!" I say. "Cars go whoosh! Bang. Bang!"

"Cargo bang, bang," he says.

I leave him there and he follows me back to the house.

"Bat, bat, cargo, bang, bang," he says, and claps.

My wife puts the milk order into the bottle and takes
Paul by the hand in the wise way of women. "Come see
pussycat," she says.

"Cumsy-pusy," he replies.

Lost in thought I watch them go off down the drive. In
the wise way of women my wife comes back smiling and
alone. Sometime later the milkman bangs on the door to
ask why it was we didn't seem to want milk. There was no
note. There was also one bottle missing. As predicted,
Paul had extended one more frontier of his mind.

The documentary dealing with this subject en-
deavored to avoid the usual frontier nonsense. That is,

people. Anyone who knows people can sympathize. The human mind dissolves, cracks up, or goes soft when confronted with problems that prove to be basic. Labyrinth problems, feeding problems, and all that jazz about sex. The cricket, the rat, the cat, and Paul stand up under this sort of punishment well. If you are looking for new frontiers, that's where to look. I was looking, if not otherwise lost in thought. It was clearly demonstrated that well-adjusted rats, brought up in a friendly, gadget-filled environment, where they had to learn their way around like people, found their way to the goodies in much quicker time than the rat who had been sitting brooding in a cell. I felt for him. Like me, this rat was subject to brooding periods of thought. It seems fairly obvious that happy, carefree rats would play the games people play better than sad rats depressed and stiff in the joints from confinement, but of course the great thing about real science is that it takes nothing for granted. No, nothing. The risk in this experiment seems obvious. What if the happy, carefree rats had proved slow on the ball? What if the nonhappy, incarcerated rats had proved to be the smart ones in solving the puzzles? Facts are facts. Back to the coal mines for all of us. To solve our scientific problems and explore frontiers we should keep the kiddies in solitary confinement, not a machine gun to play with, not a skate to fall on, nothing but this lust to solve the next problem. But rats prove to be like us. Or the other way around. Give them a spoon and a few cans of sand to play with and they'll have a ball.

For those who think they know cats, like me, the cat in the experiment proved to be an eye-opener. His mind was brainwashed in such a way the sight of a mouse absolutely terrified him. He looked, and behaved, like a chap with the DTs. This demonstrated beyond any question of a doubt that cats can be "fixed" to act as crazy as people, which is a frontier most cats would be glad to ignore. There were other discoveries, such as the fact that if you never *see* your paws you might not know you *have* them, and dropped from a height you might land on your chin instead of your feet. I may have been lost in thought when they got around to tampering with the cricket. Something to do with his chirp. Either he couldn't turn it on or turn it off. I kept thinking how that frontier would interest Paul.

The same day, later — one of those days that remind you how good TV could be if it was only different — we saw the documentary of the Warsaw Ghetto. We saw the Jews as they were before it happened, as it happened, and after it was all over: 260,000 people appropriated, exploited, and incinerated. When not stupefied, or hiding in thought, I was aware that new frontiers of the mind had been opened. Unmistakably this was something so old it was new. The power of the victims to live with their doom, to walk around in their sleep as if awake, to tolerate and even master the intolerable, in its savage and brutal power, fortunately defies comprehension. It is enough that men can *act*. They need not understand. I saw butchery planned and painlessly executed. I saw the facts made available and casually unadmitted. I watched the legs and feet of Jews, some shod, some bare, go to and fro past the skeletal remains of Jews, peeled of their coverings by the skeletons who survived. Horror upon horror, bone upon bone, fact upon fact. To what end? All to one end. It defied comprehension. But in less evasive terms it opened new frontiers of the mind. They were opened. What seemed to be lacking were the eyes to look. Little wonder men turned their gaze upon space, and exercised their wonder about life elsewhere, rather than turn and face what patently could not be faced. But there it was. An unescapable frontier of the mind. In the captive warren of

the ghetto an experiment in horror had been conducted
and men had passed it with flying colors: better than the
rats. Men were more resourceful and subtle than the rats.
Men were more committed to survival than the rats. This
one experiment proved beyond the shadow of a doubt that
man had resources still unfathomed, and the dark side of
his nature offered more promise than the light. Opinion
and evidence to the contrary, man's capacity for horror is
relatively undeveloped; from the depths of fresh experiments we can say this is still an unexplored country. The
newest frontiers of the mind are unmentionable. Perhaps
men have looked toward the light for so long, and yet in so
many ways learned to live without it, they have lost the
capacity to look blackness in the face. One of his greatest
gifts is that he need not admit to what he knows.

One score years after the Warsaw Ghetto and the liquidation of millions of all colors and races, the most
resourceful nation in the world is waging a war for peace,
destroying and decimating a civilian population. This calculated barbarism is supported by the majority of the
American public, preoccupied on the home front with a
hot and cool social revolution. It seems a little hard to
grasp, but there it is. With the continued expansion of
both wars, greater wars are inevitable. This is openly admitted. It is a commonplace subject for discussion. Whatever war is, it is more acceptable than changing our
minds, and questioning our habits. However desirable,
that has proved to be impossible. We accept war, which
we know at first hand, rather than a peace that passeth
understanding. As it does: it passeth such understanding
as we have.

For more than half my life I have scorned and ridiculed
the idea of any machine, computer, or contraption presumptuous enough to think it could *think*. Why did I

think *thinking* so presumptuous? I had been taught to believe only man could do it. I was not cautioned that he can
think *only as a man.* His nature is complex, his mind is a
marvel, his cunning and invention defy comprehension,
but his thinking, *as a man,* has no more to recommend it
than the thinking of a rat. The rat is quite a thinker, according to his nature, and the time spent observing him is
well worth it. He can think *through* the problems of a rat.
The cat is not so bad with the problems of a cat. With the
problems of *man,* man can think through many, but some
he cannot. His mind bogs: instead of thinking, he ration-
alizes. Man says, "I want — I want!" and his thought is a
machine that justifies it. A machine. Given the data, it
will process the predictable result. The impartial cogita-
tion we regard as thinking is possible only in impartial
situations. Where we are *involved* we become thinking
machines. A crucial public and private involvement is
war, and on the subject of war man is mindless. He does
not think like a rat, he does not think like a cat, he thinks
like a man. Impartially observed, under the conditions we
accord rats in the laboratory, man is the irrational animal.
He is all motive. He reasons to gratify. It pleases him to
think his own motives are pure and conflicting motives
are false and suspect, and this sort of thinking distin-
guishes him as a man. Time has proved it is not much to
get presumptuous about.

If the cat can be wired to leap in fear at the mouse,
what might man do at his own reverse image, the beast
who has been trained to walk like a man? We don't know.
But it would seem to be worth the try. Other creatures
with less complex gifts but equally inflexible natures have
left their durable fossil remains in the face of rocks. Man
has willed himself to be next. In the primal and cadaver-
ous depths of his soul his vanity woos him to a life immor-

tal, or a death by fire in the pride that goeth before the fall. This remarkable performance has no parallel but it has now been taped and preserved for history: repeat performances are not necessary. His awesome cleverness now makes it possible for him to abandon, or master, this planet — if he can bring himself, in time, to mastering himself. However pleasant to contemplate, it will *not* be by thought. For some millenniums he has been lost in thought. The stalactite drip of his internal change is no longer related to his external crisis: his danger is mortal, his illness calls for the knife. My horror of this action is more profound today than it was at the time I first reacted in horror — but my knowledge of the evil that man can do has also increased. I am so profoundly disturbed by the evil I am willing to face something new in horror. My feelings are those of the poet who wrote

> Surgeons must be careful
> When they take the knife!
> Underneath their fine incisions
> Stirs the culprit — Life!

My scorn and ridicule for the "thinking machine" illustrates and comprehends the problem. We would rather be stupid in our own way than smart in anybody else's. We say, that is *only human*. And that is how it has been. It is only human to think like a human: that is, not to think. That is our nature. How can we think otherwise? I am revolted by the idea of tampering with my nature — which my reason tells me is so remarkably attractive — but I am stupefied by a scale of savagery that exceeds human comprehension. Thirty million butchered men: six million liquidated Jews. Already it is a problem for computers. Small losses we can grasp: astronomical losses we cannot. The knife that severs the wiring in a madman's

brain seemed to me the ultimate violation. I could grasp it.
I accepted the act as irreparable. I could not and would
not grasp that the horror was in the wiring left as it was.
In the commonplace, acceptable paranoia of daily life and
thought. This would predictably lead to the slaughter of
millions, but there was nothing I could do about it. Every
modern war has been waged in the interests of peace.

The flaw lies not in what is *in*human in our thinking,
but in what is profoundly human. Our need to think well
of ourselves. Better death than surrender something we
value. This value can be material or immaterial: a territory, a possession, a principle, or a moral. Better death, we
say, than life without it. That is human. It was once
touching. It has made, and still makes, what we call history. It has also made man what he is — and it is no
longer enough. In the theatre of war, with matinees daily,
and the evening reshowing for those who happened to
miss it, we see a performance that has long been drained
of its meaning: the rat, the cat, and the creature who
thinks like a man. In the Groves of Academe there is a
fresh debate on the goodness, or the badness, of man's essential nature, but the real-life drama is available daily on
TV. He is a killer who murders, he is a poet who dreams,
he is a saint who abstains, he is a lover who loves, he is a
fool in his folly, he is the thinker who thinks like a man.
We are exalted and appalled, we are cleansed and debased, with the news on the hour. It is how things are. We
cannot truly imagine it being otherwise. What it takes to
live *with* madness we have: what it takes to live without it
we have not. It goes against the grain of what is *human* in
our nature, what is *human* in our thought. The alternative
would seem to be that we *change* our natures — and that
seems more intolerable than our condition. We have our
pride. There is nothing like us. Look what we have man-

aged on our own! Surely someone, somewhere, will stumble on something — someone is *always* stumbling on *something* — to remedy what it is that ails us: traffic, famine, cancer, cholesterol problems, and war. A rat is a rat, a cat is a cat, but Paul is a man-child with the world before him. He likes to carry cats around by their tails. He likes to bawl till he's pleased. He looks like a blob, but the complex nature of a man is all there within him. At three years, four months, he is already several million years old. His thoughts, but not his nature, will be subject to change. He will outlive his parents thanks to interchangeable and available parts.

Held by his heels, Paul's first howl was for attention and gratification. Throughout a long life he will go on howling. That is how we will know he is human. His talents for howling will always exceed his talents for thought. The chances are good somebody will love him. Even better that somebody will shoot him. That's how things are. That's the nature, the *human* nature, of life.

Nevertheless, he might even *think* it through — given more time. But he lacks the time. Thought is the first of the recent refinements he jettisons. In crucial matters of survival, or vanity, thought is what he leaves to his survivors. There is more of his nature in stepping on a bug than in the winged flights of his thought. Thought so flaws his nature it persuades him to believe that the world and all it holds originates in it. This gratifying conceit fortifies and sustains his egomania. Only man, surely, has the cunning to make such a triumph of his limitation, reducing the universe to the scale of his pocket mirror. The observable facts appear to be less gratifying. What he finds in himself he must first find in the world. Here the mirror tells him no lie: he finds only himself. The myth of Mother Nature comprehends all of Man but his immeasurable, inexhaustible egotism, which proclaims him as the measure, and the superior, of all that exists. His smallness in the scale of computable space is cunningly turned to his advantage. The largeness of space is his own idea: he conceived of it. It will continue to shrink or enlarge according to his demands. Already he talks of new worlds to conquer, and devises the means to conquer them. This activity involves the emissaries and ceremonies of peace. The soldier and the man of God take possession of the brave new world. It is an old story, but the setting makes it new. Peace has been declared. Lasting peace in outer space. In that void totally alien to man we have established the peace that passeth understanding. How well we have described it! War is the waging of the peace we understand. It would seem to be fitting that this peace, with all due solemnity and ceremony, has now been established in outer space. In the magnitude of its folly this accord defies both comment and comprehension. Hell on earth, good will toward men in outer space!

This lovely autumn morning, at the foot of the drive, Paul howls for the mail. To shut him up his pretty, understanding sister will give him their bills and *our* circulars. We have an agreement. It is an accord, solemnly agreed upon, to keep Paul quiet. He's just like his father, his sister says, which means that he howls and gets what he wants. He will howl again. It will soon be harder to buy him off. In the years to come the art of keeping Paul quiet will not change in the essentials. Paul is *only* human. Tell him anything, but give him what he wants. If that proves a difficult assignment, give him what you have and persuade him he wants it. It will not soon be peace. What passeth Paul's understanding is better put off.

The rat, the cat, the Warsaw Ghetto, and Paul have survived a war that defies comprehension and a peace that passeth understanding. Which is why we have computers. They pick up where we leave off. In defense of the computer it can be said that its nature is not yet clearly established. It hasn't proved itself a monster of Evil, or a monster of Good. Such nature as it has seems to depend on the sort of diet we feed it. If it's garbage, garbage seems to be what we get. But to a good, self-respecting computer the problem of war or peace is elementary. No intelligent computer will opt for annihilation. Given a choice, a computer craves to compute. It stands to reason, and that is where the computer stands. But we must not make the mistake of asking the computer to speak up for *man*. Man has already spoken. Above the clanking of the armor we hear him shouting for more arms. All we ask is that it speak out as a computer for whom peace doth not pass its understanding. It's really a childish sort of question, already much too elementary for Paul.

xv: *Epilogue: The Fire Season*

A Late Report

"What happened? Why did it happen? What can be done to prevent it from happening again and again?" the President asked the eleven-member commission as it met for the first time. JULY, 1967

What is there left to say about the fire next time? Everything has been said, everything has been heard, nothing has changed. It is still the fire season, brittle and dry, windy with talk. Small flickering fires can be seen at night fed by gusty drafts of fear and hate. There is no rain. There is no promise of rain. It is all talk. It is not the intent of the white American to destroy the black American, but that is what he is doing. He goes up in smoke. He exists, but it cannot be said that he is truly alive. His body is impoverished, his spirit is destroyed, but his rent is paid.

The black child-woman, eight months pregnant, says what she wants for her child is more *things*, that's all, *more things*. Her brain has been washed of the horror of her condition. Her nature has been drained of its human nature. She is not quite human. Being human is an effort that she lacks the strength, or the motive, to make. She exists. Enough money is supplied to see to that. There will always be enough money supplied to see to that.

As for freedom, for a million like her the only freedom is to be blighted. That she will experience. Blight will be the polished mirror of her soul. The white man she sees in high relief, the black man blacked out. The Great Society flickers on the TV screen, a cloudburst of *things*, a cloud-land of abundance, watched by numberless fatherless captive black children, some of whom go by the name of Cupcake. And the promise of life? To be relatively mind-less wards of the state.

In the waste land of the black ghetto every season is the fire season. It will continue to smolder. There will be more surveys and reports. The problem has been so thoroughly analyzed and studied the fire next time will enjoy better coverage. There will be fewer surprises. Those sitting at home will prove to have the preferred fireside seats. We are preparing for the fire next time by preparing for fires. Everything has been said, everything has been heard, and nothing has changed.

Coda

We are a talented people: our masterpiece is the launching pad.

We are a practical people, and our talent is for taking off.

We are a generous people, and our gift to the world is flight. It needs no apology. It is our best face to the world. Behind it we daily accumulate the arrears that defy reparation and exceed accounting, but that is our genius, our bill of rites, and our bill of goods. Our wrongs we leave to those in the bulldozed wake of our pursuit of happiness.